Food In(?)security in the South: Some possible breaking points
BY
AUGUSTINE AFULLO

CO-PUBLISHED BY
1. WAMRA TECHNOPRISES,
P.O. BOX 36665-00200, NAIROBI, KENYA
Cell: +254-722690956

2. CREATE-SPACE, USA

Printed by AMAZON, USA

© All rights reserved. No part of this publication may be reproduced, stored in a retrieval system, or transmitted in any form or by any means, electronic, mechanical, photocopying, recording or otherwise, without prior permission of the publisher and the authors.

All Photographs used in this book have been produced and processed by the authors except where acknowledged.
First published 2003
Set in Sylfaen 10/12

CITATION:
AFULLO A (2014) Food In(?)security in the South: Some possible breaking points. 2nd edition. WAMRA TECHOPRISES, NAIROBI, KENYA AND CREATESPACE ONLINE EDITION

Second edition, 2014
ISBN: 9966-7205-5-3

COPYRIGHT

© All rights reserved. No part of this publication may be reproduced, stored in a retrieval system, or transmitted in any form or by any means, electronic, mechanical, photocopying, recording or otherwise, without prior permission of the publisher and the authors.

All Photographs used in this book have been produced and processed by the author except where acknowledged.

DEDICATION

This book is dedicated to all its readers, who are committed to eradicating food shortage and hunger in the world, especially Sub-Saharan Africa.

Specifically, this book is dedicated to my Mother, Margaret Lorna Akelo Afullo, who mainstreamed food security, with a focus on ' the crops' in her life and that of her entire family, and was able to feed her 16 children to maturity, and to date, despite her advanced age (8 decades), she has maintained her farming life, and sends all her visitors with some food from her farm.

PUBLISHED BY
WAMRA TECHNOPRISES, P.O. BOX 36665-00200, NAIROBI, KENYA.
Tel: +254-722690956/ 738410345
wamra_technoprises_org@yahoo.com
Second edition, 2014
First published 2003
Set in Arial Bold 12
ISBN: 9966-7205-5-3

About The Author

Professor Augustine Afullo is an environmental health consultant, manager and trainer. He holds a doctoral (PhD) degree in Environmental science from Commonwealth Open University, British Virgin Islands (UK), a Master of Science degree in water and environmental management (MSc-WEM) from WEDC's Loughborough University, a Master of Philosophy (Mphil) degree in Environmental Health from Moi University, Eldoret, Kenya and a Bachelor of Science degree in Agriculture (BSc Agric) from the University of Nairobi, CAVS, Kabete, Kenya. Augustine has professional post-graduate qualifications in health education, environmental science, education and professional certificate qualifications in occupational safety and health (OSH) (chartered institute of environmental health (CIEH-UK)), research methods (RSA) and landscaping, ornamentals and lawn management (BCA, Botswana). Professor Afullo is a former Assistant professor in the North Central College, Naperville, Illinois, USA. He is an alumnus of the Fulbright Scholar in Residence (SIR) and commonwealth association. He is also an associate member of the African Waste and Environment Management Centre (AWEMAC), a National Environment and Management (NEMA-Kenya) registered and licensed lead expert in environmental assessment, a registered trainer in the Chartered Institute of Environmental Health (CIEH-UK), a former member of the Chartered Institute of Water and Environmental Management (UK), and the African Studies Association (ASA). Augustine has over 20 years of teaching, capacity building, training, lecturing and research experience in environmental management, education, food security, water, sanitation, and hygiene (WASH) in Eastern, Southern Africa and the United States of America. He has done many environmental impact assessments, monitoring and evaluation (M&E) tasks as the lead consultant, and supervised at least forty post graduate students in various Kenyan Universities such as Maseno, Kenyatta University and Great Lakes University of Kisumu (GLUK). Dr Afullo has published widely in refereed environment, occupational health, sanitation, hygiene, water, food and nutritional security and public health journals. Augustine is currently a reviewer of a number of academic journals as well as a member of the advisory board of the world research journal of environment and waste management.

Contents

Chapter One: Food Security — 4

Chapter Two: The Woes Of The South — 20

Chapter Three: Food Insecurity — 51

Chapter Four: The Need For Food Policy And Agricultural Review — 58

    4.01   The Risks Of Maintaining Status Quo And The Challenges Ahead — 58

    4.02   Policy Issues And Food Security — 60

    4.04   The Dawn Of A New Agrarian Era: The Reversals — 64

Section B: "The Crops" — 70

The Need For "The Crops": An Introduction — 70

Chapter Five: *Ipomoea Batatas* Sweet Potatoes — 73

Chapter Six: *Manihot Esculentum:* Cassava - Manioc – Tapioca — 89

Chapter Seven: Oil Crops: Simsim And Groundnuts — 106

    7.00   Simsim (*Sesamum Indicum)* Sesame — 106

    7.01   BACKGROUND — 106

    8.00   Groundnut (Arachis Hypogea) — 113

Chapter Nine: Pulse Crops — 129

    9.0   Cowpeas: (*Vigna Unguiculata*) — 129

'THE BALANCE OF DEVELOPMENT IN THW WORLD IS WHAT THE DEVELOPING WORLD (AFRICA) HAS NOT DONE.

THIS INCLUDES MAKING A DISCOERY TO SOLVE THE WORLD HUNGER AND MEDICINE FOR DREADED DISEASES SUCH AS HIV / AIDS.'

'THEREFORE, AFRICA…WAKE UP. IT CAN'T BE BAU.'

WISE SAYING BY: AUGUSTINE OTIENO AFULLO (OSI)…2014

CHAPTER ONE: FOOD SECURITY

Beginning is the most important part of the work (Plato- 427-327 BC)

1.00   Introduction

Food Security has to do with an all time availability of enough food of the right quality to all mankind. It is greatly affected by seasonality, income levels, distribution network, cultivation and consumption (feeding) habits of a group of people.

Food availability is greatly determined by seasonality. During and immediately after a rainy season, there is usually plenty of food for even the most deprived. As time goes by however, the supply diminishes. This can be partly attributed to large scale purchase and storage by middlemen at the time of plenty, as well as actual reduction in available volume of foodstuffs following luxurious consumption, besides other losses. The laws of demand and supply here play very crucial roles especially in as far as price determination is concerned.

When the quantity of foods available in the market suddenly falls, the prices of the remaining little shoots up. Only the economically endowed individuals then have food security. For the poor, there is no choice, they go for the foodstuff of the last resort; the cheapest. This is almost always the poorest in quality, organoleptic acceptability notwithstanding.

In the temperate world, there is a clear demarcation between the winter and summer. During the former, actual farm production, unless under forced systems, is not possible. People have to rely on the generous services of a refrigerator to survive the extremely cold and almost lifeless season. Thus in both tropical and temperate environments, there is an apparent fluctuation in food availability arising from seasonal changes. Buffer stock has to be established to absorb such shocks.

Income levels affect food security to a very large extent. A poor person or country can ill afford balanced square meals. The economic disparities, unfortunately, continue increasing in the third world where millions of people languish in the web of vicious cycle of poverty. The most deprived are most likely to sell most, if not all of their farm produce when the prices are least attractive. Thus, the product of their sweat is least paid for, exposing them to extreme shortages during other months when the foodstuffs are not only highly priced, but also scarce.

Food distribution largely relies on good transport and communication systems. An efficient network ensures a minimum cost of food, rendering it cheaply available to as many as possible. A poor distribution network only causes market inefficiencies. Poor condition of many roads in tropical world makes them impassable in some seasons. A means that can withstand such poor road conditions is most likely to be an expensive, high fuel consuming four-wheel drive vehicles. This high expense of transport has to be paid for by the end-users for the produce, the consumers. Few, if any, middlemen can afford to incur high transport expenses to avail a good product to where the demand is low. It follows automatically that the haves are likely to get enough supply of essential commodity even in critical seasons and places, at the expenses of the poor. Thus, spatial disparities in transport networking are a major cause of food unavailability in many parts of the world. In relation to this, Kenya is a very good case in point.

1.01   THE COLONIAL LINK:

The colonialists came to Kenya in the early twentieth century, and selected the cool, highland enclaves for themselves. These were the secluded areas as opposed to the rest of the country - reserves - inhabited by the Kenyan indigens. By the time these colonialists were leaving Kenya in 1960's good transport and communication network had been established in the enclaves. The hot tropical, and semiarid to marginal zones were completely discarded and disregarded. This is one reason for the famine that regularly hits these unlucky regions. It is a permanent scar that those inhabiting the hot zones of Kenya have to live with.

The subsistence economy of Uganda has been diversified right from the beginning. The Nilotes have continued relying on millet as their staple food, while the Bantu tribes, to date, rely heavily on bananas. To a large extent, these two are indigenous crops and foods in Uganda. Kenya, on other hand, was destined to be permanent home of the British - its colonial masters. It therefore took to agricultural policies that, to say the least, are unfortunately unsustainable. Its agricultural scene has, for over six decades now, been dominated by maize for Ugali, barley for beer, coffee and tea for beverage, wheat for bread, *Brassica* for vegetables and exotic cattle for beef and milk.

Time has sharpened Kenyans' taste for the above foods so much that many nutritionally superior and environmentally friendly crops and foodstuffs hitherto held in high esteem are literally at risk of extinction.

This is the main cause of Kenyans' proneness to food insecurity in the Eastern Africa region than other neighbours. The white man's foods are taken to be superior and prestigious while the indigenous ones are regarded primitive and backward. This attitude has greatly affected the demand for the otherwise superior and appropriate traditional foodstuffs that the cultivation habits have also greatly changed. To say the least, this culture of modernity is unsustainable as far as food (in)security, climate and nutrition is concerned.

1.02   EXPORT CASH CROP ECONOMY OF THE SOUTH

Most of the tropical economies are primary. This means that they heavily rely on plant - based activities such as forestry and/or agriculture for their sustenance. A majority depends on agriculture. In Kenya, agriculture has made a great contribution to the economy since the British entered the country early in the century. Though agriculture technically means field cultivation, it practically encompasses crop and livestock production both of which contribute to the food pool.

In many third world countries, agriculture supports, directly or otherwise, at least 75% of the population. It supplies food, and to play this role efficiently, food production growth rate must equal, if not exceed, the population growth rate. Agriculture also offers employment to at least 75% of the developing nations' population. To a large extent, the economies of third world rely heavily on agriculture as a provider of foreign exchange (forex). Thus, export policies tend to be much better focused and attractive than food production and internal self-sufficiency policies. This is the cause of food insecurity in these environments.

Agriculture is a source of money which many farmers rely on to build their capital base. The capital is a form of investment and stored labour. As a source of raw materials for industries, agriculture has been tremendously exploited. The tropical world is the producer of a majority of the raw materials for the North. The crops from which the raw materials are extracted, unfortunately, need the best agro-ecological zones for best marketable produce. In turn, the exporting countries get the much talked - about, much longed for forex. This has greatly enslaved the economies of the south to an extent that they have established purely export - oriented policies. This, once again, is a great threat to food security since food crop production is given secondary attention. The sector, however, supports the local industries as a provider of its raw material. Among the main cash export crops that Africa produces are coffee, Tea, Pyrethrum, Rubber, Oil Palm, Tobacco, Cocoa and horticultural crops.

1.03 COFFEE:

Is widely believed to have originated in Kaffa Province of S.W. Ethiopia. Coffee is produced for its berries which are rich in caffeine, a beverage active ingredient and a stimulant. It is a popular drink among the Europeans and Americans. It is not of any known nutritional significance other than being a source of Vitamin B (Thiamine and Riboflavin). These two nutrients, vitamins B_1 and B_2 are also found in bulk in meats, pulses and cereals. The two vitamins are needed on daily basis to the tune of 2mg by adults, with children requiring less.

Coffee requires an altitude of 600 - 1800 m ASL, a temperature of 14 - 26°C and an annual precipitation of 1000 - 2000 mm. These wide ecological ranges cover the two main species, Robusta and Arabica. The Robusta need hotter environment, more rainfall and lower altitude, while the Arabica need cooler and higher altitude zones. Fertile, deep volcanic soils are necessary. These ecological requirements of coffee very well fit to be classified as high potential areas. Coffee therefore does well in highland and upper midland humid zones (UH_{1-2}, LH_{1-2} and UM_{1-2}.)

Coffee is produced in:

1. Latin America - Brazil, Columbia, Mexico, EL Salvador, Guatemala, and Costa Rica

2. Africa - Cote D'Ivore, Ethiopia, Kenya, Malagasy, Cameroon, Uganda and Tanzania, and

3. Asia - Indonesia and India

Arabica is largely produced in Brazil and East Africa, while Robusta is produced in East Africa and West Africa. The main coffee growing zones in Kenya are Kiambu, Embu, Thika, Meru, Murang'a, Nyeri, Kisii, Subukia, Kirinyaga and Bungoma districts. The crop is exported to Europe and North America. In 1986, Kenya produced 84,500 tons of coffee. It is a protected crop which is extremely capital intensive to manage.

1.04 TEA:

A crop of Asian origin which was introduced into Europe in the 16th Century. This is a beverage crop whose leaves are rich in nicotine, tannin and caffeine. Like coffee, it has no known nutritional significance other than being a good source of vitamins B_1 and B_2. It is also a stimulant that is very popular in Europe and North America to activate cells during winter - when it is too cold.

The Assam (Indian and Sri Lanka originated) tea and Chinese (China originated) tea are produced in Africa (Kenya) and Asia (India, Bangladesh, Sri Lanka and China). Kenya tea is said to be the best in the world and constitutes 50% of Africa's tea exports. Nearly 98% of Kenya's is used for blending and improving other teas from the rest of the world. In 1986, Kenya produced 164,00 tons and earned US dollars 155 million. This boiled down to KSh. 30/kg of tea. Kenya is the third largest tea producer and exporter after India and Sri Lanka. Kenya tea constitutes 12% of the world's exports. The tea industry supports 5% rural workforce.

Tea growing in Africa started in Malawi, now the second largest producer after Kenya. Tea provides 70% of export earnings to Malawi. Tea was introduced into Kenya in 1903. The agro ecological requirements of tea are as follows:

- Precipitation of at least 1500 mm pa

- Altitude of 1000 - 1700 m ASL.

- Temperatures of 18 - 21°C, with the range exceeding 21°C not exceeding 8 months.

These correspond with agro ecological zones, lower highlands and upper midland, (LH_{1-2} and UM_{1-2}). These are found in the Kenyan highlands East and West of the Rift Valley such as Kericho, Kisii, Mau Range, Nandi, Kakamega, Vihiga, Bungoma, Sotik, Trans Nzoia, Meru, Nyeri, Nyamira, Nyambene, Murang'a, Kiambu, Thika and Embu. These are all high potential areas of Kenya. Between 1976 and 1978, East African production record of coffee and tea was as given below (in %).

Table 1: % production of coffee and tea by Kenya, Uganda and Tanzania (1976-78) Source: GOK, 1994):

Crop	Kenya	Uganda	Tanzania	TOTAL
Tea	72	12	16	100
Coffee	29	55	16	100

1.05 COCOA

Another beverage crop brought to West Africa form America. Currently, Ghana, Nigeria, Cote D'Ivoire and Cameroon produce more than 75% of all World cocoa. The rest is produced in East Indies and Central America. 5% of cocoa is produced by Togo and Equatorial Guinea. Brazil produces 20%. Cocoa's dry beans are bagged and transported overseas. Almost all is exported, as there are no processing facilities in the producing countries.

14 Ghana earns over 60% of export earnings from the crop, which it produces in over 1.2 million hectares. It is exported to Japan, Europe and America. Other cocoa production data (1976 - 78) is as follows:

Table 2: Cocoa production in Africa (x 1,000 tons) (Source: Lester B, 1987)

	1976	1977	1978
Ghana	324	280	270
Cote D' Ivoire	230	240	297
Nigeria	165	202	160
Cameroon	82	105	100

This a lowland crop that grows at 0 - 300 mm ASL. Cocoa requires at least 1500mm pa of rainfall, low relative humidity, temperatures 23 - 28°C and no long droughts. It is drought prone. It is often mixed with banana to provide shading. It is largely an equatorial crop, growing well within 10°N and 10°S of the equator. It requires fertile soils rich in iron and Potassium, but non acidic. It is exported to West Europe and North America.

Since 1970, cocoa production has not been steady due to bad weather, pathogens and neglect at the peak of the oil boom.

1.06 RUBBER

It is produced in S.E Asia, Liberia, Nigeria, Ivory Coast, Zaire, Cameroon and Sierra Leone. It was first noticed in

Amazon forest in Latin America, and introduced into West Africa. Its product is used for making vehicle tyres and carpets. It is produced in 70% of Malaysia land, more than 120,000 ha of Liberia's land as well as in Zaire. In Liberia, the rubber industry employs at least 85% of all Liberians. Rubber exports contribute 90% of Liberia's forex. The produce is exported to USA.

Rubber requires at least 1500 mm pa of precipitation, and more than 21°C of temperature, and fertile soils.

1.07   OIL PALM

This originated in West Africa and is right now produced in Nigeria, Ivory Coast (more than 80,000 ha), Ghana and Zaire. Nigeria is the centre of origin for palm oil. At least 50% of the produced oil in Nigeria is used at home, and the rest exported. Nigeria is a net importer of foods.

Oil palm requires an annual precipitation not less than 2030 mm, relatively hot environments (27°C) and high relative humidity. These are typical equatorial climates. It is a low altitude crop and needs a small range of temperature (<5°C). It is exported to UK, USA and Italy.

1.08   PYRETHRUM

This is an insecticidal crop whose leaves are rich in pyrethrene. Kenya is the main producer especially from Meru, Nyandarua, Nyeri, Kisii and Nakuru. The 1991 world demand was 15,000 metric tons of which Kenya supplied 10,500 metric tons. The produce is exported to Europe and USA. The crop needs 1000 - 1500 mm of rainfall annually, an altitude of at least 1800 M ASL, rich volcanic soils and very cool places especially highland areas. The crop needs at least 10 days of cool weather

16(15°C or less). It covers 30,000 ha in Kenya.

Kenya supplies 90% of global pyrethrum. USA and Austria are importers. Pyrethrum originated in the Palmatian Coast of Yugoslavia. It was introduced into Kenya in 1929.

1.09   TOBACCO

This originated in America. It needs 17 - 26 frost-free weeks during its production period. It needs at least 18°C and a lot of rainfall, not less than 1000 mm pa. It is a crop of lower midland and lowlands (LM_{1-3} and L_{1-2}) zones. These exist in Kitui, Meru, Tharaka, Mitunguu, Migori and Busia.

Tobacco is produced for its broad leaves that are rich in nicotine. It is used for making cigarettes largely in America and Europe. Tobacco smoking is a serious health hazard. The largest producers are USA, China, India and Russia. In Africa, Zimbabwe tops, followed by Kenya, Uganda and Malawi. It accounts for 24% of Zimbabwe's export earnings, greatly relieving it of over-depending on mining.

1.10   Characteristics of these export crops.

1)   Need the best agro-ecological zones 1 -3. They thus offer tremendous competition for suitable, high potential lands for food crops. Most often, they are given priority where a choice is to be made between any one of them and a food crop. They occupy the most premium tropical soils.

2)   Largely produced in the tropical world and exported in bulky unprocessed form to the North.

Some of the processed forms are then re-imported back to the producing countries at great costs.

3) Are greatly capital intensive, requiring fertilizer, pesticide and timely weeding treatment thereby consuming a good proportion of these resources. The food crops are therefore left least attended to in terms of protection.

4) Except palm oil, the rest do not offer any nutritionally important constituent. They also pose health hazards both in production, processing, during and after use.

5) The prices are determined by International bodies (multinationals). These are dictatorial and in most cases rather suppressive of producing countries. Most are therefore not economical to produce since the payment is discouragingly low.

6) Most countries which import these crops/produce have either their land or part of their neighbors' lands with the right ecological zones also suitable for producing these crops. However, they do not produce them because they give food production a priority in prime land allocation. The tropical world therefore remains the dumping ground for producing non -food crops.

7) The crops were introduced into the tropics by European colonists to be sure of regular supply of raw materials for their industries, thus as long as these western countries remain monopolistic consumers of these products, they are sure of supply.

8) Most are permanent tree crops, some of which cannot tolerate mixed cropping. The plantations therefore are considered permanent investments to be maintained indefinitely.

9) Most of their produce is exported to counties to which the exporting country(ies) is/are indebted. Thus, the export is viewed as a permanent link to keep a dependency relationship between the producing and the importing countries. The crop produce is also meant to earn the producing countries foreign exchange to enable them import capital (e.g. machines, agro-chemicals, etc) from the exporting countries.

10) The crops are either largely decades old plantations established by the colonialists before the exporting/producing countries got independence or their masters who left behind after independence.

To most African societies, the concept of TEA is psychological. Even sugar, charred in a pan, water added, and then sugared- is called tea. Some use tender shoots of the Black jack (*Bidens pilosa*) and the brew is still called tea. So they only produce other crops for an income which then should justify the use of the fertile land at the expense of some edible crop. So whoever buys the coffee and tea from the poor African farmer should pay reasonably for it – not peanuts .Afullo.

1.11   SUMMARY

From the above observations, it is clear that the South produce export crops largely to enable them keep a slave master bondage to which they were tied decades ago. These crops milk the soil and are extremely capital and labour intensive. They are produced in the most premium soils of the tropical world. This scenario probably sheds some light into the impending food crisis, insecurity and unavailability in these tropical and sub-tropical countries. The poorly paid for sweat of the southerners has also helped dampen their economies. These are reinforced greatly by the vagaries of nature that render the tropical world greatly disadvantaged.

A gradual shift of feeding and cultivation habits among the Southerners is believed to have worsened the lot. This change has been reinforced by biased agricultural policies of some of these countries. These have in turn greatly cheated the tropical habitants into thinking they are being modernized, ignorantly to their disadvantage and at the expense of their survival. Their economies have been rendered very fragile by being tied to very few floral resources at the neglect of more hardy and environmentally friendly crops. The few floral resources referred to here include tea, coffee, pyrethrum, tobacco, maize, wheat, barley, rice and Irish potatoes. The hardy and environmentally friendly crops referred to here include some indigenous highly nutritious products of sorghum, millet, groundnuts, Simsim, cassava, cowpeas, sweet potatoes, yams etc. When discussing these crops, Kenya to a large extent will be used as reference country. It is a serious victim of famine. However, other countries will be referred to where appropriate. For now, it is an opportune moment to briefly discuss the tropical environment and its woes to shed light into some natural causes of food insecurity.

> Men, I want you to fight vigorously and then run. And as I am a little bit lame, I am going to start running now. (General George Stedman, US army, civil war- Quoted in Mulwa F and Nguluu S (2003)

CHAPTER TWO: THE WOES OF THE SOUTH

> Whatever the ear has not heard, or the eye has not seen, the heart does not grieve about. For you cannot be concerned about a child whose crying you are not hearing.

2.00 The Tropical environment

The south lies mostly in the tropics. This is an area within the torrid zone. It lies between latitudes 23½° N and 23½° S of the equator. It covers most of Africa, most of Latin America, parts of Central America, parts of India and China. The tropical boundaries, 23½°N and 23½°S are the tropics of Cancer and Capricorn respectively and are regions of high atmospheric pressure. The equator, on the other hand, is a region of low atmospheric pressure (trough). Thus, winds tend to blow from the tropics to the equator.

Since the wind almost always follows the sun, the torrid zone experiences low pressures in about 50% of the calendar year. The sun crosses the equator twice - in March and September on its way to the tropic of Cancer and Capricorn respectively. The tropical world, most of which comprises the south, is therefore disadvantaged climatically. There are special problems thrust upon them especially the African farmer by the soil, rainfall patterns or economic situations. However, there is great potential for enhanced output. The moisture regime, growing seasons and radiation levels in tropical world suggest that crop production can have even greater potential than in the temperate world. It is only environmental conservation that should be given priority.

Due to the seasonal changes within the tropical region, there are characteristic agro-ecological implications within this region:

2.01 Bimodal rainfall: This means that there are two district rainy seasons in a year. In the northern hemisphere, (Northern tropical), these come between March and June and between July and September. In the southern hemisphere, (Southern tropics), the seasons come between September and November and between December and February.

2.02 Unreliable and erratic rainfall: The month when the tropical rainfall is expected is least predictable. Even the actual precipitation experienced then is never reliable or reproducible, rendering it very unreliable. If the rain comes, it often falls in high intensity. The total period in a year within which the rainfall is received is to the tune of 5 months. This often causes floods when the rainfall is at its peak, followed by extremely dry conditions the rest of the year. For instance on 22/3/94, Kisumu region received 60.6 mm. A total of 76.5 mm was recorded in two days. It caused floods. The El Nino rains of October 1997 - March 1998 was even worse. This is not strange in this region. According to other east African rainfall records, the Lake Victoria basin alone receives on the average more than 1 mm of rainfall per day for 121 days per year, with 198 days in a year recording thunderstorms. In Kisumu, in the 1990's, 154.9

22mm was recorded in 24 hours (the bulk of this falling in 3 hours). This shows great contrast in the same region some of whose parts receive less than 750 mm/year. With gross unreliability. Generally, Any rainfall intensity exceeding 25mm / hr is described as erosive.

2.03   Highly weathered and leached soils: Because of the high temperatures and high intensity of rainfall, the tropical soils are usually highly weathered and leached. The heat and moisture intensify the weathering process. The leached soils are in turn a result of the high amount of moisture that percolates deep beyond the rooting zones of soils. A lot of soluble salts are usually dissolved and carried down to the ground water. It is therefore common to find shallow lateritic soils in many parts of the tropics due to this leaching.

2.04   High temperatures: Tropical environments exhibit high temperatures reaching even 38°C. The lowest at times reach 15°C at night. This is partly attributable to the high tropical and equatorial insolation. These figures are shown below:

Table 3:   Insolation by region   (Source: Obara and Ogonda, 1990)

	Region	Insolation cal/cm2/day
1	Temperate 50o-60oS/N	40 - 450
2	Semi arid tropics	200 - 450
3	Equatorial 8oN-8oS	400 - 450
4	Subtropical 30 - 40oS/N	750

The insolation of the tropical region is about 2 mill. Kcal/km²/yr (8400 MJ). This makes the temperatures of this region always high throughout the year. The high temperatures cause hot climates, which increase the evaporation and transpiration losses from the surface and plants respectively. This loss therefore worsens the moisture availability in the tropics. Most of the time, there is a net moisture deficit, rendering only stress resistant or tolerant plants and animals to be able to perform well. In Botswana- in Southern Africa, there has been a record 520C recorded. The common daily maximum temperature is 32-42°C between August and February every year. Yet, solar power is not used by more than 1% of all energy requirements. This is the gold mine Africa should strive to tap and utilize- otherwise...............

2.05 High Biodiversity: due to the extremes of climatic conditions inherent in the tropics, millions of different forms of flora and fauna are / or were found in the region. Out of about 235,000 species of flowering plants in existence today, 67% are native to the tropical regions. Many however, are of unknown value and are regarded as weeds. Thus, they face serious risks of extinction. The tropical world also has the bulk of the global forest reserves whose utilization is currently being seriously debated. This rich tropical biodiversity can be used to reduce dependence on Western floral resources and technologies. New unique products can be produced and their new processing technologies devised instead.

2.06 Frequent Severe Droughts: Due to erratic

unreliable rainfall, the tropical world is frequently exposed to very severe droughts. At times, this ranges between 5 and 8 months in a year, depending on the region. It is believed that the climatic changes arising from ozone layer depletion is bound to worsen this scenario.

Drought, however, need not lead inevitably to famine if the region's natural resources are properly managed. When the ecosystems that support life on earth are over-strained, and over population and prevailing economic circumstances force unsustainable economic practices on the poor, natural disasters become most problematic. Thus proper land uses that emphasize sustainable farming systems can help cushion man from the shocks of drought.

2.07 THE TROPICAL WOES

> We must make haste. Too many people are suffering . While some make some progress, others stand still or move backwards and the gap between them is widening.......The injustice of certain situations cries for God's attention. Lacking the bare necessities of life, whose nations are under the thumb of others. Pope Paul 1967, 150)

The south has some common problems that seem unique and together they are the main causes of food insecurity in the region. This subchapter strives to clarify each one of these woes, how they are a boon to development, and how if carefully tackled, they can offer possible solutions to the myriad of problems of the South. They include:

a)   Population and population dynamics

b)   Poverty, vicious cycle and indebtedness

c)   Soil impoverishment and agrochemical use

d) Malnutrition (protein - energy) (discussed in Chapter 3)

e) Agricultural decline

f) Narrow food base.

G Aridity and desertification

2.08 POPULATION AND ITS DYNAMICS IN THE TROPICS

Table 4: Global population changes 2300 BC to 2000 AD (Source: WRI, 1996))

Year	2300 BC	800 BC	400 BC	0 BC	1650 AD	1980 AD	1996 AD	2000 AD
Population (Million)	3	5	86	133	500	4414	5700	6156

Table 5: Population growth by regions 1980 – 2000 (Source: WRI, 1996)

Region	Africa	Asia	Europe	USSR	Latin America	North America	Oceania	World
Pop 1980 (millions)	472	2563	484	266	360	247	23	4414
Pop 2000 (millions)	832	3578	521	311	595	289	30	6156
% Growth rate	2.9	1.8	0.4	0.8	2.6	0.7	1.1	1.7

The tropical (Asia, Latin America and Africa) populations are estimated to double in 20 - 25 years. Africa's population doubles in 24 years; Asia in 39 years and Latin America in 26 years. This is a great threat to mankind, given the un-matching food production growth rates. Each year the global population increases by more than 90 million of which Africa contributes 12 million. It is estimated that going by this trend, there will be at least 6.1 billion people globally by the year 2000. Of this, 80% (4.9 billion) will be in developing tropical world.

This trend is worrying, given that more than 50% of the rural population in the tropics are unable to have the minimum food requirements due to poverty. The record food production for the 600 million people living in Sub-Saharan Africa has been dismal. Kenya, for instance, is projected to have a population of 36.9 million by the year 2000, going by the current annual growth rate of 3.6%. Its population and food production growth rates have never matched since 1970's. This is almost the same trend globally. This is shown in the table below.

Table 6: Population and food growth rates 1950's - 1990's. Global and Kenyan Case (Source: Lenilian and Fletcher, 1977)

Years	1960's	1970's	1980's	1990's	1950's	1960's	1970's	'80's	90's
Population growth rate %	3.3	3.9	3.8	2.7	2.2	2	1.90	1.75	1.51
Food production rate %	2.0	3.6	3.4	1.4	3.1	2.6	2.2	2.0	1.8
Region/ Level	Kenya				Global				

Whereas the global food scene looks bright, it is unfortunate that food production growth rate always trails the population growth rate in Africa. This calls for an increase in food production by 40% annually for the next 2 decades. Otherwise, if there is sufficient food, population can as well be left to grow undeterred.

2.09 Population Dynamics

Generally, young, well-educated people in the tropical world, Kenya included, shun agriculture. They prefer to go for white-collar jobs in urban areas. This is largely because agriculture has a low status in the minds of many young people. Few are interested in it. They assume that the dirty rural farmers, a majority of whom are poor and lack opportunities, have their survival threatened. The young therefore want to try their luck elsewhere.

In Kenya, 15.5 million (i.e. 60% of the population) are young people below 25 years of age. Of this, slightly above 30%, 4% and 0.3 % are in primary, secondary and post secondary training institutions respectively. Another 4 million are either unemployed or undertaking small-scale income generating activities in rural and urban areas.

2.10 Urban Rural Migration: Causes explained.

Inherent in colonialism was the premise that western ways were superior to the African ways. This marked the birth of a misconception that good things come from the west and everything else is inferior. This notion stifled indigenous innovations and confidence. Thus, anything that was traditionally part of the African society was disregarded by the increasingly educated lot. This was the beginning of the fall of the agriculture sector, and with it food security. The sector's growth was greatly stifled, reducing the momentum of evolution of some of the traditional activities.

Agriculture, right from the colonial days in Kenya was only important in the colonial enclaves. These were secluded white mans' land which had very conducive farming environments. There were resources, infrastructure, cheap labour and suitable ecological zones to top the resources up. Management was the willing type, which believed in maximum profits.

Due to forced labour, many Africans preferred to forever evade the farming environment. Thus many of those who started going to school right then were simply seeing the school as a place from where one eventually came out with an academic Jembe. This was true especially of those who hailed from climatically disadvantaged parts of Africa. In Kenya, many Luo community youths were taken to school with this motive. No wonder, very few, if any were taking agriculture courses at secondary and professional levels. Instead, they flocked fields such as engineering, medicine and law. Even the currently popular commerce was greatly despised.

In general, therefore, many communities in Africa looked down upon Agriculture as a profession of failures and farming as a job of the uneducated (i.e. those who never went to school). Thus, many school leavers were simply given a chance to go and live with their relatives in urban centers, where they would get a white-collar job. It was never imagined that anybody who had gone to school could ever came back home and do farming regardless of scale and motive. Therefore, whereas most youths are better educated than their parents are, this same education is seen as a better reason for them not to engage in agriculture. Therefore, the parents, as elderly and weak as they are, prefer to be left alone at home. They see no need to assist their young sons and daughters with resources such as to enable them fully employ themselves in farms. The youths themselves are even more withdrawn.

It is for this reason that there is, almost every year, a labour deficit in all parts of Kenya during peak crop seasons. It becomes a serious constraint during cultivation, planting, weeding and harvesting. Even the scale of farming is too low since only elderly labour is utilized and the young energetic labour idle. However, Kenya and many tropical countries are basically agricultural. They thus need to strive to utilize such idling resources as the youths. Deliberate and planned absorption of skilled youth into the sector can help ease unemployment since white-collar jobs no longer exist in towns. Establishments of cottage industries can greatly help sort the mess. Rural indigenous technology is very handy here.

There is an urgent need to provide the farmers with land ownership documents such as title deeds. Then supportive services such as credit schemes can be devised so that the farmers use the title deeds as loaning collateral. This can enable even those with very small

30 parcels of land to rent or lease some for crop production, rear stock, market or process agricultural commodities.

> Poor people are rarely met. When they are met, they often do not speak. When they do speak, they are often cautious and deferential, and what they say is often either not listened to, or brushed aside, or interpreted in a bad light. Chambers Robert, (1983)

Rural lives are associated with poverty and lack of opportunities. The very fact that the life there is abhorred means that very few, if any, regular earners can freely associate with it. Thus, the rural conditions need to be improved so that youth can be attracted there. Transport, communication, entertainment (and other social amenities), water, farm input stores, among other services need to be strategically placed in the rural environments to attract all classes of farmers, especially the youth to develop the rural areas. As long as the rural area and the youth are neglected, there is bound to be more rural poverty and rural brain drain. The attractive lifestyles in the urban areas will trap the youths who in turn will be tempted to even go abroad, worsening the brain drain in developing countries.

In Kenya, Siaya and Homa-bay districts lead in out migration. This partly accounts for the poverty in those districts. In a place with limited productive resources such as labour and skill, no marketable goods and services can be produced. Thus, no money or capital can be attracted. The region thus remains poor. Due to the urban trap of the indigenous elites of such an area, there is no market for even the limited local farm produce. Thus the prices remain low and help keep the production at subsistence level since there is no incentive to increase production. Thus permanent poverty is what the tropical world faces if it continues allowing brain drain.

2.11 POVERTY, VICIOUS CYCLE AND INDEBTEDNESS.

Many tropical countries are greatly indebted to the North. In Africa, there are countries with an unsustainable debt mountain, urgently needing debt relief. 18 countries are most poorly placed, while another 12, including Tanzania, could easily fall into that category in future. Most of these countries heavily rely on agricultural export crops to service their debts as well as earn forex. They are already caught up in a web of poverty. Poverty is a state of complete deprivation, with clusters of disadvantages interlocking to produce a syndrome called vicious cycle of poverty. The clusters of disadvantages are powerlessness, vulnerability, physical weakness, poverty itself and isolation. Poverty, however, is a strong determinant of the other factors. It contributes to physical weakness, through lack of food; malnutrition leading to low immune response to infections and inability to have health services.

Poverty, therefore, denies people access to food since they lack power to purchase it from available markets. The state of physical weakness arising from malnutrition worsens the situation since the poor become less productive. Due to lack of opportunities in many parts of the tropical world, brain drain has been the order of the day. Those with less purchasing power stay behind. Being largely the poor, they desperately look for market for their farm produce. More often, the more informed outsiders who are also better endowed economically, come in to help the situation. They become monopolistic buyers of a produce that ends up fetching dismally to the producers.

At times, the produce can be ear marked for export to service foreign debts. The debts are part of resources given out by the better-endowed economies to poorer countries. In the state of extreme desperation, the latter readily accept to be offered a loan, grant or aid. This slowly accumulates. They become unserviceable, as is currently the case with 18 countries in the South. The borrowings, however, never improve the economies of the recipient countries, least of all, the receiving departments. This entangles the borrower to greater need for more resources to help finish up already started projects.

As the debt burden grows, the recipient country becomes worried about its inability to pay back. Noting this state of helplessness, the contributing economies "agree to sit down with the debtors and talk". Here they assess all possible means of repayment, and get to know all economic secrets of the indebted countries. They then propose to be exporting produce to the owed country as a means of servicing the debts. The importing country then dictates the prices of this import, ending up paying poorly for the poor countries sweat.

Thus a permanent, skewed, economic inter - dependency bond is created. The exporting, debt - burdened, countries become slaves and make policies to declare such an export crop protected. Thus permanent crop plantations have to be established to cement the slave - master farms. Any of the following amount to negligence / neglect of the crop:

- Being infested with weeds, in whatever scale.

- Being infested with pests to any scale.

- Being infested with diseases and pathogens of any magnitude, mix and kind.

- Being intercropped, i.e. being produced in the same field with any other crop. Any sign of neglect exposes one to being charged in a court for a serious offense. Once charged, the "suspect" is liable to a number of years' imprisonment or a heavy fine. Yet, this law was left behind by the colonialists over 3 decades ago. One would wonder why it is still operational after such a long time when this can only be that the crop was a bond to keep an economic relationship for use in servicing the never ending debts Kenya owes the North

2.12. SOIL HEALTH AND YIELD DECINE

Fertilizer use in the tropics

A study by Tropical Soils Biology and Fertility Unit (FAO) found in 1996 that Kenya's fertilizer use is only 37% of what it should be. Even then, it is only confined to commercial farms and export crops. Of the subsistence farmers who grow 75% of the country's food, 98% use little or no fertilizer. This is largely because they cannot afford it.

Kenya uses 285,00 tons of fertilizer per annum. This is largely imported from European Union, Italy and Japan.

Each importing country provides fertilizer as grant - in - kind for the crop whose produce it imports. i.e. for the crop, it has bonded to service its debts. Thus 33% of 1996 Japanese grant to Kenya was meant for agrochemicals. The total amounted to Kshs. 1.56 billion. The same year, Italy gave grant of 7,000 tons of fertilizer for Tea and Coffee production. Every year, donor funded programs account for at least 80% of pesticides supplied in Kenya.

Depending on their economic position, commercial farms also operate at three levels:

1. There are those who do not apply fertilizers at all;

2. Those using up to 100 Kg nitrogenous and 100 Kg phosphate fertilizer per hectare; and

3. Those using between 100 and 250 Kg of nitrogenous and the same quantity of Phosphatic fertilizer per hectare. Those which do not apply any fertilizer utilize very fertile soils, which are at times virgin. This is applicable to the Nyayo tea zones established in 1980's and 1990's for which forests were cleared.

Other than Zimbabwe (before the land crisis came up) and South Africa, almost all other countries of the south import the fertilizer they use. A few Sub-Saharan African countries have commercial deposits of rock phosphate but lack the necessary capacity to manufacture fertilizer from it.

Due to the import costs, sub-optimal levels of fertilizers are applied in the south. FAO figures (1983) indicate a 7.4 kg/person/yr (19.5 kg/ha) use of mineral fertilizer in Africa. The corresponding levels in the north and globally are 65.5 kg/person/yr (114.8 kg/ha) and 25.5 kg/person/yr (78.5/ha) respectively.

2.13 The need for fertilizer use: land degradation and soil impoverishment

The high rainfall intensity, leaching and other characteristics of tropical soils have already been mentioned. However many other factors come together to reinforce the need for fertilizer application on these otherwise moisture-deficient soils. Erosion and leaching are too high in the tropics. They together cause soil nutrient loses equivalent to 1.5 billion pounds per annum. This is thrice the fertilizer equivalent used in Zimbabwe annually.

In 1 ha, up to 700 kg of N, 450kg K and 1000 kg of P are lost annually from soils of the Sub-Saharan Africa. This loss is attributed to erosion and leaching. In many parts of Africa, continuous cropping with maize has compounded the problems. This is because maize has an open growth that leaves the soil exposed to threats of erosion. Thus in a maize monoculture farm, 80 kg of N and 18 kg of P are lost annually (per season) per hectare. These nutrients are removed as grain and stalks which leave the soil as food and feed or fuel respectively. This therefore explains the need for adding nutrients to the soil after harvesting if the same is to be re-used immediately. In Kenya, for instance, between 196,000 and 240,000 tons were used annually in the 1990's (Yusuf, 1987)

It is notable that of the 16 or so essential nutrients for growing plants, the least available in African soils is P. It is, however, the least susceptible to leaching since it is largely immobile, with long soil persistence. The most soluble of the nutrients, Nitrogen, is lost most by leaching, followed by potassium. It is therefore not a surprise that many underground water reservoirs in Africa are saline, having dissolved many salts on their way from the ground surface.

As far as erosion is concerned, deforestation and cultivation are responsible for most of the soil loses. It is estimated that 20 -50 tons of topsoil is removed per hectare on an annual basis from African soils. These soils are cropped continuously with little or no external addition of nutrients, decreasing their ability to sustain crops. There used to be 4 - 5 decades of fallowness to give the soils a rest for replenishment. Right now, the cropping intensity has increased so much, even at times to 100% that there is hardly recovery time for soils. Thus a total 742 million hectares of land in African have been rendered almost useless for agriculture. In 1990, Global Land Degradation Study (GLASO) found out that between 1945 and 1990, at least 15% of the global land was degraded either beyond restoration or so badly damaged that only major engineering works could revive its full productivity. This is a worrying scenario, given the burgeoning global population. The world watch Institute estimates that the worldwide loss of topsoil exceeds the rate of formation by 24.4 billion tons per year. In Nigeria, cassava planted on land of 1% slope lost 3 metric tons of soil /ha/year; on a 5% slope lost 87 metric tons, while 15 % slope lost 221tons. The loss associated with 15% slope is equivalent to rate of soil formation in 10 years.

It has already been noted that many inorganic fertilizers are hardly affordable to the majority of farmers in the south. This, coupled with the long-term effects on soils and water-bodies, render the inorganic fertilizer technology an inappropriate one in the tropical world. Alternatives have to be sought, and urgently so. The impending food insecurity on the tropical world unfortunately has reached its peak 3 - 4 decades after the advent of green revolution. This calls for immediate action.

To rejuvenate the soils, some agro-forestry trees and shrubs have been highly recommended by ICRAF. One such example is hedgerow plant, *Tithonia diversifolia*. Although not a leguminous plant, it has high nitrogen of up to 3% in the leaves. *Lantana camara* also proves more phosphorous in their leaves than most other plants. Whereas most plants have 0.1% P in the leaves, the *Lantana* spp contains thrice this much. It is thought that the roots of these plants may be mycorrhizal. The use of the leaves of these plants for mulching is capable of doubling and even trebling crop yields. It has also been noted that the use of *Sesbania Sesban* as an agro forestry tree reduces *striga* spp (witch weed) infestations of fields. This is a parasitic weed which germinates and attaches to the roots of larger grain cereals such as maize and sorghum from which it derives all nutrients.

Human existence depends on, among other things, the top 30 cm layer of the earth's crust. Combined effects of soil erosion, exhaustion from non-sustainable agricultural practices and, to some extent, deforestation have resulted in severe desertification.

2.14 DESERTIFICATION, ARIDITY AND CLIMATIC CHANGE

Desertification is the encroachment of large areas of barren land, which are covered with sand, uncultivable, lacking vegetation and largely uninhabitable in the more productive and habitable regions. It arises from aridity. Aridity, on the other hand, is the state of the soil or land being dry, barren and lacking sufficient moisture to support vegetation.

The Sahara extends across the African continent from Senegal to Ethiopia within an area called Sahel. The Sahara is extending southwards, resulting in major displacement southwards of the poor climatic zones. Already parts of Kenya are affected seriously. The desert is encroaching in the other lands at the rate of 8 - 10 km per annum. Each year, 6 million hectares of formerly productive land is reduced to sand. A further 21 million hectares are reduced to a condition of zero productivity.

For dry areas, the value of land being lost is estimated at 26 million US dollars. Wind erosion is most serious in marginal, transitional and ASAL areas. Desertification affects nearly 1 billion people (17% of global population).
It occurs in 70% of the dryland or ¼ of the total land area of the world. It costs the world more than 40 billion US dollars in lost productivity with 65% of this attributed to actual land value loss. Up to 1350 million ha (30% of the world's ASAL's) are already facing desertification. 67% of the degraded lands are found in the south, largely Asia and Africa. This is critical because in Africa, ²/₃ of the continent is desert or ASAL, and 73% of the agricultural dryland are already seriously or moderately degraded.

The great deserts of the world are located in the zones of atmospheric high pressure. These flank the tropics at about 30°N and 30°S latitude. They extend pole ward in the interior of the large continents. Many have less than 10 cm per annum of rainfall. Extensive deserts are located in the North Africa, Southern part of the African continent; in the near East; in Western, North and South America; and in Australia. Less than 5% of North America is desert. There is no known desert in Europe. The South therefore, has fragile and dry lands that need full protection and careful use for long - term benefit of the inhabitants.

Desertification has worsened poverty in Africa. It has led to out migrations to urban centres, and at times, to Western countries. Instead of running away from our own problems, we need to sort them out. The evasive approach has compounded food insecurity, since unsustainable cultivation and feeding habits have been carelessly aped from the west. Yet the climate is not conducive. An overview of the food production records in the south will shed more light into this.

Table 7: Kenya agro - ecological zone classification (Source IGAAD 1990)

ZONE	Mean annual rainfall (mm)	Land area ha (000)	% of total land area	Cumulative %	Classification potential	Climatic class
7	Rainfall <150	-	0	0	None	Desert
6	< 300	10,573	18.4	18.4	Very low	Arid
5	300 - 500	27,041	47.4	65.8	Low	Semi Arid
4	500 -700	7,314	12.8	78.6	Low to Medium	Marginal
3	700 -800	2,426	4.3	82.9	Medium	Semi Humid
2	800 -1000	3,296	5.8	88.7	High to Medium	Sub Humid
1	> 1000	6,407	11.2	99.9	High	Humid
0	Other	1733	0.1	100		
	Total	58790	100	100		

. 11,530 ha (17.1 %) high and medium potential zones 1 - 3

. 12% is transitional (zone 4)

. 46140 ha (65.8%) low potential (ASAL) zone 5 - 6

2.15 KENYA'S NARROW FOOD PRODUCTION AND CONSUMPTION BASE

Kenya relies heavily on maize, wheat, rice and Irish potato as staple foods scene. Below is a crop-by-crop production data and position in the current Kenyan food.

Table 8: Regional 3 – The "Great Cereals"' Production in Kenya (1992) in 000 tons Source: GK, 1992)

Province	Central	Coast	Eastern	Nairobi	NEP	Nyanza	Rift Valley	Western
Maize	177.8	95.7	498.1	2.5	1.2	490.8	1245	540
Wheat	6.4	-	18.2	-	-	-	284.9	0.2
Rice	3.2	8.9	-	-	0.1	11.1	-	2.5

2.16 MAIZE:

It is a high-potential-land crop from which to expect reasonable yields. Extremely low yielding varieties survive well in dryland areas (ASALS). Needs 800 - 1545 mm pa; 18 - 27° C and very fertile soils. In Kenya, it is produced in the Rift Valley and parts of central Kenya - Nakuru, Bungoma, Kakamega, Trans Nzoia, Nandi, Uasin Gishu and Marakwet districts. Maize yields here are the highest in the country.

The production of this crop in Kenya increased by an average 4.4% pa between 1963 and 1973. This was the first decade of Kenya's independence. Since then, production has greatly dwindled. Between 1980 and 1990, there was only a marginal increase in maize production. However, the situation worsened since 1991, with the import bill increasing annually.

By 1994, crop forecast and food supply showed the lowest grain production in 10 years. This coincided with previous records of 1993/94 as being the worst drought and food insecurity period Kenya had ever faced in 50 years. Thus, the maize imports shot from 128,740 tons to 650,387 tons within the 1993-94 period. An equally high amount of wheat and rice were imported, with the previous imports being almost trebled in each case. Nobody even thought of alternative crops and foods of the dryland. Within this same critical period, the highest sugar, skimmed milk powder, cooking fat and oils imports were recorded.

Maize consumption in Kenya is projected to grow to 40 million bags (3.6 million tons) by the year 2000. Many Kenyans (southerners) go for it. If it is not available, then normally the government declares a food crisis (famine) period and an import signal is switched on. India produces the crop very intensively to suffice its needs. In the 1994/5 period, it produced 192 million tons, enough to feed its over 870 million inhabitants. This was attributed to heavy chemical inputs, using even those globally declared environment health hazards decades ago.

The current food crisis in many Sub-Saharan African countries is attributed to the narrow subsistence sector and sharp taste for maize. It is a high potential crop whose production in export crop producing countries has greatly dwindled. It has been relegated to the periphery, compared to cash crops.

In the 1960's and 1970's maize production growth rate was 2.5 and 4.7% (global) and 2.4% and 3.1% (Kenya) respectively. For Kenya, these valves were far below the population growth rate of 3.3 -3.9%.

2.17 WHEAT:

This grows best in temperate regions of the world. It is produced in large quantities and with high efficiency in Australia, former Soviet Union and United States. The economies of scale greatly enhance their efficiency. In Kenya, 1 ton is produced at 15,560/= while in US, it is produced at 12,537/= and in Argentina it is 9,625/=. India also produces wheat efficiently albeit of what is feared to be lower quality. It is affected at times by Karnal bunt fungus which causes yield losses and affect grain quality. However, they still proudly feed on what they produce.

Canada currently produces 20 million tons of wheat in 10 million hectares. The Northern Africa wheat yields average 670 kg/ha, while Western Europe yields 5 tons/ha. Kenya's yield is around 1 ton/ha. There seems to be no prospects of improving Kenya's production since it is associated with large-scale plantation farming and high capital outlay. Thus, it remains a preserve of the rich, who have an access to a combine harvester. By 1989, the first and senior most Kenyan National University, the university of Nairobi had only one "stalled" combine harvester, yet in the same period, the private Narok, Mau Narok, Keiyo and Uasin Gishu wheat and barely farms had the same machines ranging to tens - live and operational.

Thus the monopolistic nature of cultivation of this crop renders its market in Kenya very inefficient. Kenya only produces Durum wheat, which is also grown in Ethiopia, India and Egypt. This variety grows in relatively dryland regions; have higher straw; heat resistant, but susceptible to rust. It is soft wheat used for making paste, baking cakes and other soft wheat products.

The other regions, USA, Canada, Argentina, South Africa, Australia, Portugal, USSR etc. produce the hard wheat of the variety Triticale. It has short vegetative growth, long reproductive growth, high quality and high yield. The hard wheat does not crack on baking cakes and other soft wheat products. Since Kenya's wheat is almost entirely soft, it has to source the hard - wheat requirements from the North. Its annual wheat production ranges between 250,000 and 300,000t, against an annual demand of over 700,000t. The short fall is made good by imports. The crop is hardy, requiring 300 -1015 mm pa of precipitation and 6 - 20°C. It is a hardy crop sown in well prepared lands in June and harvested in October. In North Africa, it is cultivated in the more temperate Morocco and Algeria. The bulk is produced in Russia, USA, Canada, France and India (In that order).

Wheat is the greatest cereal in global output with 387 million tons produced annually. Rice is the next with 367 million tons annual output, although it is the most widely utilized (fed-on) cereal.

In the 1961/66 period, Kenya imported 0.5 million Kenya pounds worth of wheat. This amounted to 1% of the country's total foreign earnings. The trend has remained to date, but on a worsening side. More and more of the forex is being used to meet import requirements of selected cereals. The high proportion of these cereals imported in the total food imports of the African countries tends to reflect not a relative failure of indigenous staple food production, but a partial shift from locally produced foodstuffs.

In the 1960's and 70's global wheat production growth rate was 2.7 and 3.5% respectively. Kenya's production was negligible on global scale.

2.18   RICE:

Origin Asia. This is a water-loving crop that needs 1145 - 1780 mm pa for good yields. There are, however dryland rice varieties that need less water. It is also a heat-loving crop performing best at 20-27^0 C. It is an indigenous tropical crop having originated in either India or China, both in Asia.

30% of China's land is under rice and this produces 40% of the world's output. China produces 36% of all rice of the world. China and India produces rice for local consumption whereas Thailand exports a lot. In Thailand about 50% of the land is under rice. Other chief producing countries include Indonesia, Bangladesh and Japan. Tanzania produces 75% of East African rice.

In Kenya, it is produced largely in the great Kano plains in Nyanza province under irrigation. Currently only 52,000 ha are being utilized whereas the total irrigable land in Kenya is over 540,000 ha. There is also a clean, reliable water source Lake Victoria. Besides, the Kano plain is a large stretch of flat land, which can conveniently serve for irrigation use. This is only a wish, which can only be operational with political and economic will.

The production of rice in Kenya is coordinated by the National Irrigation Board (NIB), a government parastatal.

The production inefficiencies are just but unbearable. Thus, the NIB tenants get less financial returns than their freelance rice-producing neighbors do. Secondly, the current production of rice in the two main Kano plain schemes - West Kano and Ahero is unsustainable due to the pollution of the water sources and the soil. There is too much fertilizer input which has greatly impoverished the irrigated soils. The concerns about environmental sustainability, conservation and management of natural resources have become a first priority. Unfortunately, the world is increasingly becoming complacent to them, the increased awareness notwithstanding.

Rice is one of the most important crops of the world. It gives a higher production of food per hectare than any other crop and can be grown every year in the same field without decline in yields. About 50% of the world's population, especially in Asia, depends on rice as the main food. China and India produce more than 50% of world rice. No wonder, they are most populous sub-continents, yet still able to feed themselves-unassisted.

2.19   IRISH POTATO (POTATO):

A crop of the rift valley, western and central parts of Kenya. In 1995, Nakuru district alone produced 89,000 tons and 1994 about 93,000 tons. Nakuru, Narok, Uasin Gishu are the main producers of the crop nationally. 17 districts in the rift valley produced in 1993, 1994 and 1995 a total of 156,000t, 20300t and 290,000t respectively. The average yield is 12 -15 t/ha.

The main hindrance to increased production are bacterial diseases (soft rot), poorly available seed, poor producer prices, fungal disease etc. ADC (Agricultural

Development Corporation) is the only seed producer in the country, but only produces 10% of farmers requirements. Very frequently, bacterial diseases destroy seeds in the Molo store, yet this prides to have the best potato storage facility in Africa.

The crop has great nutrient demands from the soil. Heavy fertilizer application is therefore inevitable. It is a cool season crop which needs $15 - 20^0$ C, and at least 1000 mm pa of rainfall uniformly distributed over the 4 month growing period of the crop. Unfortunately, Kenyan's taste has preferred this potato so much to the neglect and expense of other root and tuber crops. There is an urgent need to broaden the feeding habit so that the dryland root and tuber crops can also have their own niche in the food market of Kenya. These include cassava and sweet potatoes.

Already there is competition for land between this crop and others which need high potential prime land for good yields. An emphasis should be shifted and urgently laid to crops that can produce well in dryland zones which is 80% of Kenya. The El Nino and Lanina phenomena are already too clear to Kenyans.

2.20 SUMMARY

The risks of utilizing these few food resources - wheat, barely, maize, rice and Irish potatoes are adverse. Traditional crops, foods and livestock species are giving away to HYVs and breeds very fast. As plant and animal breeding is all about selection and manipulation of genetic resources, the traditional genetic resources of the south are at a great risk of extinction. As the genetic base of plants and other resources become narrow, some genetic material is irretrievably lost. This rate of loss exposes 5- 10 % million species to risks of extinction by the year 2000. This is about 10 - 20 % of global genetic resources. In 1960's and 1970's, Kenya's potato production growth rate was 1.2 and 3.9 % respectively. This falls far below the demands.

Table 9:   Maize: production and import Records in Kenya (1975 - 95) (Source: GOK- 1996)

Year	75	76	77	78	79	80	81	82	83	87	88	89	90	91	92	93	94	95
Yield (bags/ha)													18	19.8	19.1	14.5	22.7	20
Exports (000 tons)	120.8	113.2	8.14	23.4	120.5	.020	.94	.95	122.5									
Prod. (000 tons)										651.9	485.3	525.7	509.3	303.5	515.2	241.8	316.0	
Imports (000 tons)	.357	.032	.032	.080	.018	323.9	77.4	89.1	-	-	-	.002	-	-	415	128	650	630

(Blank spaces means records not available)

Table 10: Kenya's Wheat & Rice production and import data (1986 - 95)

Year		1986	1987	1988	1989	1990	1991	1992	1993	1994	1995
WHEAT	Production (tons)	309700	148300	220200	233200	78500	199000	175000	76900	105200	330000
	Import (tons)	115281	217857	75578	123200	322632	241612	100808	314400	353076	350000
RICE	Production (tons)	25800	30100	14738	16206	20004	15207	16206	13603	10999	
	Imports (tons)	61745	39129	10000	30000	27983	61163	58920	37150	93519	

CHAPTER THREE : FOOD INSECURITY

3.01 INTRODUCTION

Having gone through the tropical woes, the cash crop dependence, the tropical climate and the narrow subsistence sector, it is important to discuss at this juncture the result of all these: food insecurity. Food Insecurity is largely attributable to the narrow genetic pool for food, (i.e. only very few food crops are overemphasized); significant climatic changes; inappropriate policies; untapped irrigation potential; indebtedness; slavery to international policies; and poverty.

3.02 The actual food scene in the south.

Kenya has one of the lowest food security levels internationally. 46% of the rural population (about 13 million people) lives below the poverty line. This is considered an income level below Kshs 1852.90 (US dollars 36 per month). Thus only very few can afford to purchase foodstuffs even if it were available in the markets. The national cereal production and import records in the 1980's and 1990's show that the future holds more challenges than promises. By the year 2025, Kenya's population will be over 50 million. This means that food production will have to increase by at least 75% for the next 3 decades if "food for all" is to be regarded as an attainable goal. In the early 1970's, chronic hunger and malnutrition was affecting 80 million people in Africa. In 1989, the number was 10 million and the rate of growth of the population continued to seriously exceed that of food production. Many traditional agricultural systems that were ecologically stable only 5 decades ago are breaking down now under this intense population pressure.

Since 1970's, Africa's rate of population growth has been maintained at 3.2% pa, the fastest than any other region in the world. Food production, on the other hand fell about 12% between 1965 and 1982. In the North, food production rose by between 6% and 49% pa in the same period. Thus, a good proportion of the Africans are increasingly being exposed to risks of food insecurity. The pathetic income growth rates worsen this already gloomy picture. The world food scene was rather stable for the period 1960 - 1980. For instance, agricultural growth rate was 2.3% globally while Kenya's was 2% (1960's) and 3.2% (1970's). Maize production growth rate was 2.5% (1960's) and 4.7% (1970's) in Kenya against a population growth rate of 3.3 - 3.9%. Sweet potato, cassava, sorghum and millet production growth rate over the whole period fell drastically. This could be a direct effect of modernization and green revolution.

It looks like the recorded global per capita food production growth rate of 22.32% is seriously misleading since Africa records a negative rate. The other countries of the south record an average of 6% while the North records 49%.

3.03   Food aid to the South.

It is estimated that food deficit in Sub-Saharan Africa will shoot a peak of 90 million tons of cereals by the year 2005. This is going by the 1990 deficit level of 10 million tons. The global cereal supplies are becoming tighter. Food aid availability is therefore likely to shrink and keep intensifying. Increased cereal prices and reduced food availability to many therefore look an obvious result. There is an annual 9.5 million ton drop in aggregate cereal production globally. This partly explains the shrink in food aid availability from the North. Cereal import bill is likely to increase by US dollars 1.4 billion p.a. for the south. This is sure to worsen indebtedness. Despite this, FAO calls for a 3% annual increase in pesticide use up to the year 2000. This is to enable the world achieve the motto of "food for all by the year 2000". The North has been giving food aid to the south for many decades now. At the moment, we seem to have reached a point where any extra food aid seems not to be of suitable help. Thus the marginal utility to food aid is almost negligible. Yet food insecurity is worsening every day. The very fact that the food stocks of the North available for aid is depleting, with no signs of satisfaction from the south means a new strategy has to be sought. The North is tired with the South: the latter has proved a heavy burden courageously carried by the North. The South should realize this fact. They need to understand that if they were also contributing positively to the food market, food availability could have greatly improved globally. The global food deficits seem to be a gap, widening day after day, for the South to fill. The South has never sat down to utilize its resources to help it boost its food availability. They have to sit, think and act in a way to fill the food gap. The North has done its best. They are currently tired of this continued aid and the south should read the signs of the times well.

3.04   Populations actually at risk of undernourishment.

About 800 million are perennially hungry in the world. It is estimated that 40% of Africa's population suffer from hunger. This is significant given the continent contains 12% of the global population. Up to 9 million people face severe food shortages in the horn of Africa. In addition, an estimated 22 million people in Africa are faced with food emergencies. In the 1984 - 85 famous African famine, one million people died while 10 - 12 million became environmental refugees. Then in 1993, the same number died, this time in Sub-Saharan Africa alone.

Between 1980 and 1998, up to 100 million extra people have become perennially hungry, adding to the 700 million that used to be there. Thus as effective demand for cereals is expected to be 2800 million tons by the year 2000 for 6.1 billion people. Achieving this demand, going by the current level of operation in agriculture, looks a tall order. This is worsened by the fact that within the last 2 decades, global per capita food availability has been in the decline. In early 1980's, this decline affected 37 countries of which 24 were in Africa. This trend seems to be maintained, since FAO (1996) reported that Africa was then the only continent where per capita food production was declining. In the horn of Africa, cereal production declined by 5% pa in 1990's. Wars and desertification are worsening the scenario. The 1985/6 period recorded an annual deficit of cereal grains in developing countries of between 100 and 200 million tons. This number has increased tremendously. The deficit should be regarded as a gap that the south needs to fill, i.e. the challenges ahead. For before the deficits which largely affect the south are filled, the affected countries will always remain under-developed. This is a great threat to mankind. The African will be extinct if care is not put in.

All those living below poverty line are highly susceptible to undernourishment. By 1993, this population was 844 million globally. Of this, Sub-Saharan Africa had 26%, South East Asia 62% and Latin America 12%. A well-fed population is very healthy. A healthy nation exhibits high productivity in any activity the citizens engage in. This is bound to not only increase national income, but also reduce the medical bill that the country spends.

3.05   Malnutrition in the South.

This is the main acute physical expression of absolute poverty. In 1993, the number of seriously malnourished globally was 520 million people. Energy malnutrition means any feeding program that offers one less than 1520 Kilocalories/day. Whereas this is the most vulnerable group, it is not all. A 1966 FAO survey report (1963 - 64) in Nigeria showed that available supplies of calories of 2719 Kilocalories per person per day and 80 g of protein/person/day provided adequate nutrition. Thus those getting between 1520 and 2719 K calories/day are very vulnerable to malnutrition. In many parts of Africa, between 1774 K calories and 1909 K calories is consumed per person daily. This is clearly deficient.

With respect to proteins, between 33 grams and 40 grams is commonly consumed per day in Africa. These are grossly inadequate, rendering most Africans prone to protein malnutrition. The global per

capita protein consumption is 43 kg per annum, while it is only 26 kg in Africa. In terms of age groups, children are most malnourished in the south. Adults are much better placed. In children, the malnourishment level is all time high in Africa, with about 33% suffering to some degree. It is widely accepted fact that the home of malnutrition is sub-Saharan Africa. As a result, 30% of Africa's children are underweight, while it is 9% for South Africa. The % of underweight children in sub-Saharan Africa has been an average of 30 in sub-Saharan Africa with the actual levels being 29%, 30% and 31% in 1985, 1986 and 1995 respectively. Kenya is among some 9 countries where malnutrition is on the rise. This affects 23% of Kenya's children. Even though Asia produces a lot of food, rendering it almost self - sufficient, it has its own special nutritional deficiencies. 50% of the world's malnourished children are found in only 3 of South Asia's countries - Bangladesh, India and Pakistan. 50% of children in southern Asia are malnourished. From this scenario, it is evident that malnutrition due to food imbalance is much more common a problem than hunger. India's level of cereal production especially rice and wheat is so high that in 1995/6, it produced more than enough for its 870 million inhabitants. Kenya imported some of India's surplus cereals in 1996. If such a sub-continent can face malnutrition, it means that there is great need to review food production and consumption policies in the south. The south in general and Africa in particular is the centre and land of malnutrition. 69% of Africa's population lacks the basic needs for minimum diet, seriously escalating the malnutrition, especially protein. Policy reviews can help play the trick.

East African Standard, Thursday, 23/10/1997 pg 6 by Okech kendo.

Okech kendo gives an account of how African politicians and policy makers best approach poverty alleviation. His article is entitled:

...reflections: Activities of International day of eradication of poverty.

He says.......... Breakfast at Inter-continental Hotel, Lunch at Hilton Hotel, tea at new Stanley Hotel, and Dinner at Grand regency Hotel - all on a day set aside by the United Nations (UN) to remind the world, peoples and governments **that it is possible to eradicate poverty.**

Breakfast began with a glass of juice and fruits to build the mood. A waiter was on standby asking: What can I give you, Sir – Tea or coffee?

In front of me was a heap, rolls of bread of diverse shape, texture, quality and taste. I could make a return journey to passion, orange or pineapple if I wanted. If I didn't feel like any of the liquids, I could ask the waiter for something else.

There was an assuring voice of the host: feel free to make an order for the breakfast – toasted bread, pallets of bacons, sausages, eggs, boiled or scorched potatoes, and the lot were the details.

As the **poverty fighters feasted** on a breakfast whose price was enough to buy food for a poor family for a week, and a saving, there was talk on poverty.

Yet a child wants just enough to buy uji and githeri at a construction site- and .... adds the author.....1 US$ for a week would be a treat of a lifetime. The street boys may even want to make such a generous mdozi the next president.

(Uji means soft porridge; Githeri means cooked mixture of beans and maize; Mdozi means boss.

With this approach to life, there is only one solution- a change in a big way.

CHAPTER FOUR: THE NEED FOR FOOD POLICY AND AGRICULTURAL REVIEW

> No people can profitably be helped under institutions which are not the outcome of their own character. Edward Blyden-Black American living in Liberia, 1903)

4.00 INTRODUCTION

Lack of enough of the right kind of food by the south is already clear. The world can no longer shut its eyes to the already disturbing situation. Every year, governments and international organizations meet to "reaffirm" their commitment to the principle of "food for all". They need to do more than just reaffirm principles; there seems to be more promises than action on the global markets. These promises can only be fulfilled if there is cereal and food/subsistence market. The problem of eradicating hunger is political, not just nutritional, technical or economic. There is thus a need to shift focus from national and international economic developments and growth indicators to the more basic, home grown, need oriented, and household food self sufficiency. Poverty is the underlying cause of food insecurity. It must be addressed through improved socio-economic performance. A country whose populace has a high per capita income is sure to be better fed both quantity- and quality- wise. This cannot only enhance disease resistance but also higher productivity. Productive workers deserve a decent pay, and thus can be better customers.

4.01 The Risks of Maintaining Status Quo and the Challenges Ahead.

In the face of competition from exotic varieties,

indigenous foods are slowly but surely being eliminated from Kenyans' diet. Many traditional foods have high nutritional value. However, they no longer appeal to a large section of Kenyans, and the third world in general. This could be attributed to inadequate research. It is not just food production patterns that have changed. Food consumption patterns are changing from traditional food crops because their processing has been little researched. Therefore, we need to shift our agrarian processing to rural areas where the priority is processing of traditional crops as opposed to the exotic ones. At the global level, world food discussions have tended to concentrate on seven crops - wheat, barley, maize, potatoes, rice, beans and oats. These have dominated the scene and to them, various international research institutions are designated. Much indigenous food crop development in the south has therefore rested on the hands of local farmers rather than research institutions. A few countries of the North have little biodiversity in agricultural crops but strong gene technological industry. Africa, on the other hand, has rich genetic agricultural resources, rendering them genetically diverse. To widen their genetic base, the North has secretly taken away some of Africa's genetic resources that it uses in biotechnology and breeding. Already, some African communities have come up with new crop/plant variants and have added to parts of biodiversity. They should therefore not be considered as mere observers and conservers of plant genetic resources.

It is therefore not a surprise that 1996 world food summit in Rome, with a theme of "food for all by the year 2000", convened to discuss food security and nutrition, never agreed on the final biodiversity text. In Africa's biodiversity in agricultural resources lies its economic strength. The sooner it realises and institutionalizes this, the better.

4.02 Policy Issues and Food Security

The neglect and abandonment of traditional foodstuffs is perpetrated nationally by the lack of policies and programs to promote and support the preservation and consumption of indigenous foods. This applies well to Kenya. So serious is this national tragedy that Kenya often imports or seeks relief food aid even when the country actually has store full of traditional cereals like millets and sorghum. This has helped narrow down Kenyan diet to maize, beans and potatoes. Thus it has worsened dependence on imported cereals such as wheat.

The Kenya sessional paper No. 1 (1986) listed 7 commodities as central to achieving development goals and targets established for agriculture. These were coffee, tea, maize, wheat, milk, meat and horticultural crops. The crops listed as secondary included sorghum, millet, rice, root crops, sugar and oil crops. The criteria used in this rating took into account factors such as:

- area under the crop
- market value of the crop
- importance of the crop in creating employment for rural populations- contribution of crop to food security and nutrition- forex earnings

The horticultural crops listed in other popular government documents include fruits and vegetables. The fruits include passion fruit, citrus fruits, avocado, oranges, mangoes and bananas. The vegetables include European and Asian vegetables such as Lady's Fingers (Okra), Dudhi, Karella, and Chillies. These are exported to Europe, America and Asia.

In 1990, KARI, Kenya governments' chief agricultural research body came up with a crops' research priority rating list that was quite wanting. It showed a clear bias towards exotic crops at the expense of indigenous hardy nutritionally superior crops. Thus, the bias against 'indigenous' crops and food resources in Africa seem to have had a deep foundation of formalization. This is clear in many governments policy documents. So far there is little research which has been designed to improve the quality of food crops in Africa, and the South in general especially from nutritional point of view.

Despite the much resources assigned for research in exotic food crops, they are still closely matched, and even outweighed in yield and quality by the least researched indigenous crops of the south. The marginal returns to research in exotic foods and crops are already negligible. Why can't we develop a will to positively view the indigenous foods and crops of the South? In their raw, un-researched form, they show yield and nutritional superiority. Why can't we assign them some research resources? Their yield and nutritional response potential is sure to surprise many. They should be given a chance. Their genetic advance is bound to be impressive.

The paradox of local food insecurity is that while we in Kenya have ploughed most of research resources to improve wheat yield, we have never achieved even 1 ton/ha. The North gets 5 t/ha. Kenya is contented with a potato yield of 12 t/ha, and does not seem to be bothered. The North targets a marginal yield per hectare of 1.0 tons despite the fact that it already gets over 20t/ha of the crop. Similarly, the North with already full internal self-sufficiency in food, targets a 1.8 t/ha marginal yield in corn production. Kenya, most affected by chronic food deficits, seems contented with 2 t/ha as the average national yield.

What seems clear is that Africa becomes contented with too little, even in the middle of a crisis. The North is more worried about having enough feed for its livestock and pets. The main worries they have are risks of obesity, heart attack, high blood cholesterol levels and other diseases and conditions of the affluent. The lifestyles of the North are already luxurious. It is therefore a contradiction that they can rely on the south for supply of cash crops for their industries, while the latter languish in poverty and malnutrition. We have for too long been contented with sparing our prime lands for these protected crops to maintain the slavery.

It is high time the African and the South at large said "NO, enough is enough", have a break and reflect. A wise reflection will tell us to resort to our traditional/indigenous food crops - millet, sorghum, cassava, yams, sweet potatoes, pulse, crops, oil crops and indigenous vegetables '(weeds)'. A reversal is simply inevitable.

4.03   The inevitability of reversals

That food scientists should come up with food substitutes for use during shortages is an obvious fact. Yet we have already known the substitutes. We should stop looking for who has not done and needs to do what; we have no time to make a balance sheet of who is responsible for what. Losing such precious time means we will all die (those in the south). In fact, they should be declared threatened species. While past research had long revealed that less available foods like the traditional ones had immerse potential, this has not been adequately exploited as an alternative source of food. We have dearly paid for this neglect and more payment is sure to be demanded due to inaction.

Thus, the paradox of food abundance and scarcity in the same country such as Kenya is a situation which depict food security policies that do not augur well for all. While many parts of Kenya have surplus foods, a good part of the year, arid parts are ravaged by famine largely because of drought. The crops, which can best do in, such marginal environments (80% of Kenya) are well known and continue being marginalised. The marginalisation has now been institutionalized - we have to continue serving foreign (the North) luxury needs for beverage and other forms of 'balanced diet' at the expense of our empty stomachs.

Free famine relief food has become a 'lingua franca' in many parts of Kenya. In Marakwet district - Kapsowar area, the residents (indigens) simply cluster around the NCPU depot in west corner every day between 9 am and 4 p.m. - from August to February every year. Farmers harvest in November and December and the region, other than the hotter Kerio Valley (Tot and Aror regions) is high agricultural potential. After the free maize is given out, the 'famine stricken Kapsowarians/Marakwets" go to the nearest posh mill and sell the same at the market price to the immigrants. What a paradox! Whatever is harvested (yield 30 bags/ha) is sold to the NCPU only to be re-acquired free the following 'famine season'. We surely need to change our attitude; we need to make a revolutionary reversal - in attitude and action.

The 'lingua franca' also applies in Eastern province - Kamba-land. One concerned resident had this to say publicly as reported in a Kenya daily newspaper on 22/9/96 page 14 (special report);......"and because virtually all rely on relief food intervention, only a few plough their farms when the rains come. The people are used to food handouts. They do not do anything when the rains come, but sit back and expect the government to provide....."During the peak famine period of 1996/97, some famine-stricken people in Kamba-land, Kenya, had to remove the remains of a week-old dead dog from its 'grave' in order to get a meal.

4.04   The Dawn of a New Agrarian Era: The Reversals

The proposed reversals are at two levels - personal and institutional

4.05   Personal reversal: the do's and don'ts:

- Learn to consume what is produced immediately around your 'home'. "Home is where you live".
- Learn to produce what best does in your environment - crops or livestock that are best adapted to your local climate
- Plant some crop with any rain that falls. Some only need one heavy rain to establish. Do not waste rain.
- Keep livestock size that your own plot can support. Do not trespass with your livestock to your neighbours.

- Eat what is meant to benefit your body, not luxurious ones that cause diseases of the affluent.

- As much as possible, eat what is produced in your own country to promote its market.

- Use any means to preserve all sorts of foods to reduce wastages. It is better even to import preservation technologies for local use than import preserved foods.

4.06   Institutional Reversals

These involve the government policies which need to be urgently revolutionalised - "a revolutionary policy shift". It should be noted right here that the revolutionary changes could be most risky, given their abrupcy. Most risky ventures are also known to be most lucrative in terms of results and returns. It all means a short-term sacrifice -investing - with hopes of establishing a stronger, more sustainable foundation of our economics. Some areas of immediate need for policy shift are:

*1.   Change agricultural policies from export biased and based to subsistence- local food sufficiency based. This could mean starting to under crop cash crop fields with food crops - the fittest can be left to survive. With time, however, a complete change to food crops is inevitable to reduce competition from export crops.

THOOOOOOO!!!!! MIAHA.

Miaha is a LUO name for a newly married (wed) bride. The Luo are a Nilotic community living to the west of Kenya within the Lake Victoria basin (Nyanza Province).In the traditional Luo system, a bride had to be given a piece of land under her care, use and custody. This was a sign of recognition, acceptance and respect. At the same time, a woman acquired more respect from her ability to produce food, for it was then guaranteed that her household (and perhaps the entire homestead) would never starve. However, producing food was simple and easy. All one needed to do was to go to the plot intended for whatever activity- be it clearing, digging, planting, weeding and so forth, walk around the plot marking the boundary where you wanted the activity done, then use your tool to just hit once - AND NO MORE, THEN LEAVE. The field would then "do itself" in your absence, exactly following the boundary marked, and clearing- if that is what the owner intended or wanted done- and so forth. So work was easy- all that was needed was initiative.

Hard-working women were highly respected, upto their homes. When their people visited, they would be assured of very high level and warm reception. So newly wed ladies would start to look for , hoping to earn this level of respect by impressing their in-laws. So a number would go out of their way to have it. However, there were always induction courses (orientation) they would be given by selected senior women of the community. These included teachings about taboos, do's and dont's. However, even in a class, however much a teacher tries, it does not always go to 100% pass.

In one such an attempt to impress her new in laws, one bride (miaha) broke this cardinal rule of farming. She went to her field, followed the normal ritual of marking the boundary of the plot she wanted to have dug, but messed up by using the hoe (hitting the ground)more than once to dig the plot. When she left the plot, she, as usual, expected that the rest of the work would "do itself". But alas! When she came back, the plot was as she left it. The community was informed of the development, and when they went to check where she had hit the ground, it was realized to have been done more than once. Since that time, the community had to toil, and do everything. If you start digging, the work will not move until you sweat for it, and it will remain at the exact point you leave it for you to come and continue.

When the community realized this new development, they could only curse the bride who brought the misfortune to them - and therefore the exclamation- Thooooooo! Miaha!. To this day, the LUO have to toil to get food. Life has never been the same again for this fish- loving Nilotic community.

*2. Encourage each citizen -farmer- to have at least some land under a suitable food crop that is proven does best on that ecological zone-; comparative advantage should be utilised as far as farm layout is concerned. This then spills over its effects to land use.

*3. Encourage the cultivation of drought resistant crops. This is where the saviour of 'Kenya - the country' lies. Produce enough dryland foods to suffice the entire country in the currently idle 80 % of the land.

*4. Discourage non-essential exports, and only cultivate few export crops. Most of the prime land - formerly European enclaves - should be spared for food crops.

*5. Learn to say "No" when offered aid that simply enslaves your country. Aid meant to maintain the export crop on prime land- is a fake, insensible and insensitive aid. You can do without it.

*6. Practice more domestic polices than international policies; we thus need to develop a domestic policy base with known standards and criteria which we can use to assess the performance.

*7. Learn to utilize available floral and plant genetic resources as opposed to the old practice of importing all sorts of materials including AIDS viruses.

*8. Collect and research on all traditional food and alcoholic drinks, and their processing and preservation methods. The quality standards of these resources should be set nationally, and any that meets such standards left to be freely utilised by citizens. In them lies the base for industrial development and take off. The industrial sector needs to be fully liberalized so that the fittest will survive, while giving some modest protection to rural industries

*9. Lastly, establish agricultural policies that clearly outline and emphasis the use of dryland. Here dryland crops should be encouraged. The dryland crops and their production offer future hope for the economies of the south. Climatic changes are bound to intensify global warming. Thus with time, as the globe warms up, more heat tolerant crops will need to be emphasised. We need to start now.

*10. Look for import substitutes for edible oils and fats, as well as pulses, etc. Some important crops considered primary for development of the economies of the south are discussed one by one. They include:

♦ Cereal crops - millets and sorghum (presented in another volume).

♦ Pulse crops - cowpeas, beans and grams

♦ Oil crops - Simsim, groundnuts, sunflower, rapeseed, castor oil plant.

- Root and tuber crops - cassava, sweet potatoes, yams

- Indigenous vegetables - 'weeds' (presented in another separate book).

Total reliance on a mix of the above enables one to have a fully balanced diet with all dietary constituents such as vitamins, minerals, energy, essential fatty acids, essential amino acids and other micro-nutrients. Special attention is given to the fact that most of these crops can do well in hot, dry climate, even with 400 mm pa, Ceteris paribus. Thus, the final policy shift requirement is to change the National Agricultural pointer towards them, so that they become the centre in the third world agriculture.

SECTION B: "THE CROPS "

.Sorghum .Millet .Cassava .Sweet Potatoes
.Groundnuts .Simsim .Cowpeas.

The need for "the crops": An introduction.

The results of the past agrarian practices in the South are chilling. The South has been getting food aid since the exotic foods and crops were introduced. It has however continued having more intense food insecurity - hunger and malnutrition.

* Even in continents and countries of the south where the green revolution picked up, the diseases of poverty have continued being major problems. There is thus a need to have alternatives or a better mix.

* The economies of the south have continued worsening - languishing in indebtedness to the north. The causes of the debts have to be assessed and alternatives sought to ease stopping of increasing debts.

* We have more untapped resources than what we pay heavily for to import from the North.

* Those in our midst who have been traditional in their feeding habits die at very advanced ages - 90's or over. The modernized die very early.

* Modern lifestyles of the North can only be maintained by large sums of money, they are

luxuriously expensive. The south does not have such resources to sustain a susceptible and fragile family.

* It is only a service and/or good that one can sustainably produce in one's own long-term home (or permanent environment) that can ensure sustainable income and source of living.

* Green revolution technologies cannot be successfully adopted amidst poverty. Poverty alleviation techniques have to be devised before the green revolution can be adopted.

* The north has contributed greatly to technological advance and food. The gaps left seem unfillable unless the south takes the initiative to face the challenges.

* Most of the south is dryland and desertification is fast encroaching, coupled with climatic change. We should read the signs early and adopt heat-loving crops before the changes eliminate us.

CONCLUSION

In the 18th and 19th centuries, development of agricultural enterprises in the topics was stimulated by demand from the north (Europe) for agricultural raw materials for their industries. Since independence, however, the tropical inhabitants have continued getting poorer. The poor cannot even offer a market for their own locally produced products and foodstuffs. Thus, an improvement of the standard of living of a people may lead to greater consumption of their own output of a product. Increasing per capita incomes can therefore be a sure way of curbing the looming poverty especially in sub-Saharan Africa. Asia seems to be improving every day in terms of economic placement and poverty alleviation. The south and East Asia regions are good cases in point, having recorded impressive economic growth rates in the last 3 decades. This same region had some of the poorest people in the world more than 30 years ago. Africa then seemed to be much better off. It could be worth conducting a research to disapprove this theory:

> "A state of equilibrium in African peasant agriculture has been assumed to have established for a very long time. In equilibrium, there is no incentive to expand production. Therefore to improve the food production and growth rates, the system has to be disrupted by changing the market prices and food production techniques."

CHAPTER FIVE: *Ipomoea batatas* Sweet potatoes

5.0 HISTORICAL BACKGROUND

5.01 Origin(s)

Sweet potatoes, Ipomoea batatas, originated in Central America west of the Andes Mountains and parts of Latin America. These were also the centres of diversity.

5.02 DOMESTICATION AND SPREAD

It is believed that Ipomoea batatas was domesticated at the centres of origin. During the 16th Century, the new crops, one of which the crop is, were spreading throughout the tropics. By the Precambrian times, it had reached Polynesia. The sweet potato capsules are thought to have crossed the Pacific Ocean by floating from the Western Coast of the Americas to Asia. Human migrations intensified the crop introduction to other parts of the world, especially as part of trade.

In the Eastern African region, the origins look mysterious. The Luo of Kenya inhabiting Nyanza Province, believe that the crop was introduced at the Nyanza Lake shores by a type of Hippo called Nyaundi. This Hippo is believed to have deposited the crop capsules with its stool. The `seeds' then germinated into attractive crops that were very much liked by goats. Human beings living along the lake then became curious, and coupled with craze for food gathering, they decided to start uprooting the sweet potatoes. To their dismay, it had well developed tubers underground. They started using the tubers in different forms, and finally fully took it as part of their food. They started cultivating it.

From the Pacific Ocean and Lake Victoria associations of sweet potatoes, it is clear that the crop has been widely spread via water-bodies. The crop is now a stable crop among many African and Asian communities. Only the two continents commercially produce the crop, with Africa producing 4% and Asia 92% of the total global production.

5.04 ECONOMIC IMPORTANCE

Sweet potato is the only economically important species of the more than 400 tropical members of the Ipomoea genus. It is of convolvulaceae family.

Its tubers are a staple food among many in the sub-Saharan Africa, as well as Asia. The vines are used as livestock feed in many parts of the highland and temperate regions. Its tubers are also a source of raw material for many industries. The leaves are an important source of vitamins and minerals when utilized as vegetables. Once established, the crop needs minimum attention.

5.05 ECOLOGICAL REQUIREMENTS

Ipomoea batatas requires a warm climate of at least 20°C throughout the season. This is best available in areas of altitudes less than 1500 m above sea level. It does best as a tuber crop within the tropical region 30°N and 30°S of the equator.

The crop requires between 750mm and 1000mm pa of precipitation. Of this, at least 500mm should be available during the active growing period. Sweet potatoes withstand drought, but low yields are experienced if drought strikes within the first 6 weeks of planting. This period is critical because tuberization occurs between the 4th and the 7th week of planting. The rest of the period is simply for tuber enlargement.

Figure 5: Pictures of some of the crops discussed in this chapter.

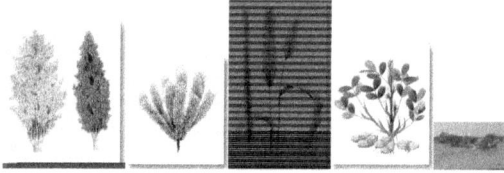

Roots, which normally grow to 20cm - 2m deep, develop into tubers as a result of secondary growth. There are very few roots within the top 20-25cm.

Sweet potato does well in a wide range of soils - from sandy to sandy loam to clay loam. However, it is very susceptible to waterlogging, thereby rendering clay soils unsuitable for its production. The crop is a short-day plant requiring at most 13.5 hours of daylight in order to flower. This is typical of most tropical crops, most of which are either short-day or day-neutral. Tuberization promotes vine development, a quality also promoted by low temperatures. Since the latter is typical of highland or temperate environments, sweet potatoes for vine yield is very common in such cool, high altitude areas.

Day-length of at most 11 hours promote flowering. Since the critical yield component is the tuber, flowering is an insignificant phenomenon. Vines also act as planting material thereby rendering seed production and therefore reproductive growth merely a luxury. However, for production of new varieties with desirable traits, seed production in selected environments such as research institutions and seed multiplication centres can still be encouraged.

5.06   CROP ESTABLISHMENT

After thorough primary and secondary cultivation, the field is ready for sweet potato planting. Vines are used. The crop is unusual in the ease with which it can be propagated successfully. Apical cuttings of vine are used, and planted with 50-75% of their length buried.

Crops establish whether their basal or apical ends of the cuttings are buried. The cuttings, usually 23-90cm long, are planted on flat land, ridges or mounds. Vines are placed 30-60cm apart in ridges 90-150cm apart, or 4 or 5 vines placed in mounds 1m apart.

The decision on whether to plant the sweet potato vines on mounds, ridges or flat land depends on many factors. These include soil depth, water table, drainage and cropping system. Sweet potato needs deep soils. Therefore, any soil that is less than 2m deep needs establishment of either mounds or ridges to avail enough pliable soil easily penetrated by the roots.

The main function of plant roots is moisture absorption. The drier an environment is, the less the soil moisture and therefore the need for more elaborate root systems. A plant in a waterlogged soil therefore is liable to produce very weak root system. Since sweet potato tubers are simply enlarged roots, the roots need to have a sub-optimal soil moisture content to establish in large numbers. The stage that needs more moisture is tuberization - the enlargement or secondary thickening of the already established roots. Thus waterlogging is a hindrance to good tuber establishment if high tuber yield is the desired goal.

5.07   FIELD OPERATIONS

Application of farmyard manure (FYM) is the main known field operation. It improves yields tremendously. The fact that no inorganic fertilizer is recommended for application in a sweet potato field implies that it is very likely that such a research has never been conducted. Being largely a tropical and therefore a poor-man's crop, sweet potato seems to have had minimum research attention both nationally and internationally.

The next essential field operation is weed control. Any form of wild or volunteer growth typical of tropical countries is found in a potato field. These are better controlled within the first one month of planting. The second month is very useful as far as tuberization is concerned. Thus the developing roots should be left intact from the second month. Sweet potato is very sensitive to weeding shocks it gets from the second month. After the second month, however, there is no need bothering about weeds. This is because sweet potato is a very effective fast growing cover crop which fast smothers any weeds. It is therefore hard to come by weeds in a well-established and timely wed sweet potato field by the third month.

Traditionally, the crop was established as an under-crop in a cereal field. It was planted after weeding the main crop. Cultivation of sweet potatoes is relatively labour saving. No other known field operation is undertaken other than weeding and FYM application. However, some light earthing up can be done to ensure that any tubers getting exposed to the soil surface due to soil displacement is covered. This saves them from being preyed on by man or rodents. Earthing up also reduces chances of the tubers becoming fibrous. Fibres develop in tubers if the soil temperature and therefore, moisture content is not stable. Direct heat from the sun exposes a tuber to a false stimulus of drought, thereby making it fibrous. This is an undesirable quality. Lastly, earthing up is done to ease tuber expansion.

5.08 DISTRIBUTION IN KENYA, AFRICA AND GLOBALLY

In Kenya, sweet potato is popularly cultivated and utilized as a staple food by the Luo and Luhya of Western Kenya. Even though the crop is of tropical American origin, it has become so much part and parcel of these two communities to the extent that it can be regarded indigenous. Historical association of a Hippo, Nyaundi, with the crop among the Luo is all telling. A viable part of the crop is believed to have been deposited together with the hippo stool at the Lakeshores. This live part germinated, produced a crop that the Luo only took to as a staple food out of curiosity and craze for gathering. It was soon domesticated, and taken to by the neighboring Bantu tribes such as the Luhya and the Abagusii. To date, it is a household crop in many parts of Kenya, especially in the lowlands. It, however, predominates in Nyanza and Western provinces. It is cultivated in parts of Central province for vine as livestock feed.

5.09   HARVESTING, STORAGE AND YIELD(S)

Africa used to produce 5% and Asia 95% of the total global sweet potato production in 1970s. However, in 1980s Africa dropped to 4% and Asia 96%, produced in 11% and 85% of the total land areas respectively.

In Asia, Korea is the major and most efficient sweet potato producer. The yields there average 16.3 tons/ha, while the global yield is 8.3 ton/ha. Africa's yield is a limping 3.9 tons/ha. Among other producing countries, sweet potato field yield range between 2.5 and 50 tons/ha. The high yield potential, coupled with high calorific density, render sweet potatoes a great famine - reserve crop. It is no wonder, therefore that it is popular to many.

Being sweet, it has good organoleptic acceptability. It also has disease, pest and drought resistance once established. This has made it popular globally. The advantages should be used positively to promote its production and yield. Harvesting is done by either uprooting the entire crop or removing individual tubers piece-meal. The crop is ready when the soil is seen cracking, showing the pressure exerted to the soil by a mature or fast expanding tuber. By opening up the cracks a little, the tubers can be either harvested or re-buried, depending on their sizes.

Due to their succulent nature, sweet potato tubers have a short shelf life. However, they can keep for long if exposed to a temperature of 27-29.5 $°$ C and relative humidity of 85-90% for between 4-7days, then stored at 13-16°C at 85-90% Relative humidity. Drying and chopping can also improve their storage qualities.

5.10 GROWTH HABITS AND VARIETIES OF SWEET POTATOES

There are numerous sweet potato varieties, a majority of which are only traditionally known. Those with extensive shoot systems even in soils considered suitable for tuber establishment normally have poor tuber yields. They therefore best serve as livestock feeds especially the vines. Then there is a second more popular type among communities that consider sweet potato a staple food. This type has less shoot but elaborate root system from which tubers develop. Generally, the crop is a trailing vine with sweet, succulent tubers.

The tubers are of different shapes, sizes and colours depending on the variety. Known varieties include Sifwembe, Nyakarika, Nyamayare, Nyaguta, Nyamilambo, Olombo jopidi. These varieties can again be classified on basis of their nature or colour of flesh and / or skin. The skin colour can be white, brown, yellow or red. The flesh colour, on the other hand, can be purple, white, yellow or a mixture. The sweet potato varieties can further be classified on basis of nature of the tuber flesh. The first group has a firm, dry mealy flesh after cooking. The second group has soft moist gelatinous flesh after cooking, while the third group has very course tuber only suitable for industrial use or livestock feed.

5.11 CHEMICAL COMPOSITION AND USES OF SWEET POTATOES

Sweet potato tubers have the following composition: (mg/100g fresh weight)

- ⇒ Ether extract (fats and oils) - 1.8-6.4mg,

- ⇒ Moisture content - 50-81mg

- ⇒ Starch - 8-29mg (25% amylose, 75% amylopectin)

- ⇒ Protein - 0.95-2.4mg; at times up to 39% crude proteins. (Protein comprises 2/3globulin has no

   tryptophan and sulphur amino acids)

- ⇒ Reducing sugars - 0.5-2.5mg,

- ⇒ Calcium - 200mg; Iron - 3.0mg

- ⇒ Thiamine - 0.1mg; Nicotinic acid - 0.9mg

- ⇒ Carotene - 1-1.2mg; Riboflavin - 0.06-0.17mg

- ⇒ Ascorbic acid - 29-40mg.

- ⇒ Provides 7.4 million calories per hectare, with 96 kg protein/ha.

When boiled, sweet potato tubers become sweeter. This is because much of the available starch is converted into sucrose, making it sugary. This happens readily because much of the starch is in the easily hydrolysed amylopectin form and only 1/4 in the amylose form.

The sweetness of the tubers and vines expose them to pest attack. Thus, their shelf lives are relatively short. To cope with these weakness while capitalising on the sweetness of the tubers, a number of processing techniques have been introduced. These techniques are closely related to the uses to which the tubers are put.

The tubers are often washed and boiled or chopped and boiled. It becomes soft and sweeter, a form in which it is readily used for breakfast with liquids such as tea or porridge. It can be used also for major meals such as lunch and supper.

At times, traditionally, the Luo of Kenya used to chop, dry and grind the sweet potato tubers. The flour could then be mixed with that of other grains such as millet, sorghum and/or cassava and used for making any form of gruel or traditional brew. Any form of drink thus made from sweet potato powder was called 'AMARA' by the Luo.

When harvested and not to be put into immediate use, the sweet potatoes traditionally used to be preserved in different other ways. The intact uninjured tubers could be put into holes dug about 1m deep and covered with the soil. In that state, the tubers could keep for long, and only removed piece-meal for use. This method could at times be necessary during famine when it could be deemed necessary to harvest the entire crop from the field to save it from being stolen. Otherwise, field storage was a popular method among the Luo. In this method, harvesting was only done piece-meal as need arose.

Yet another method of keeping harvested tubers involved washing, chopping and drying. In this form, the tubers could be soaked and boiled or ground depending on the intended use. These sweet potato processing technologies and uses are known by both Luhya and Luo communities of Western Kenya, some Uganda and Tanzania communities bordering Kenya. The crop thus seems to have deep association with Lake Victoria basin. The vines of sweet potatoes are used both as planting material and/or livestock feed.

5.12 BOTTLENECKS TO SWEET POTATO PRODUCTION:

i) The main pests of sweet potatoes include:

   a) Squirrels and monkeys - eat tubers

   b) Sweet potato weevil (Cylas) produces a vine and tuber-burrowing larvae, causing bitterness and odd colours of tubers. They also open up wounds for secondary infection by other pests and pathogens.

ii) The main diseases include:

   a) Virus - B disease is transmitted by whiteflies (Bemissia spp). This causes distortions of the leaves, especially at the shoot apex, greatly reducing photosynthetic surface area and yield.

   There are virus resistant potato varieties

that can be effectively used against virus-B disease. In addition, control of whiteflies using any means is essential. There are many varieties resistant both to the disease and potato weevil. The knowledge of these remains a preserve of the traditional sweet potato producing and consuming communities.

iii) Besides the pests and disease, perishability is the next main problem of sweet potato production. There are varieties that cannot keep in the soil for long once they are ready. They either rot or become prone to Cylas Spp attack. Some tubers also crack, a sign of either irregular moisture availability and/or over maturity.

iv) The last main bottleneck to sweet potato production is lack of appropriate planting material. The crop is drought escaping as it has a very short productive life, therefore maturing very fast once planted on time. In the short run, therefore, there is sufficient tuber production. In Kenya, sweet potato production as a staple crop is practiced in the lowland zones very prone to environmental excesses such as droughts and floods. Thus, long droughts can easily render useless all the vines leading to an acute shortage of planting material in the next season. The weevil-infested vines are even more prone to drought.

At the onset of rains, it takes time to assemble sufficient planting material, frequently delaying planting in such areas. This tends to render ineffective integrated pest management (IPM) methods as the most environmentally friendly component - the cultural method is already compromised. The time lapse therefore significantly reduces crop yields, as the birch effect does not benefit them, besides other advantages of early planting. These problems call for research in a number of areas.

5.13 KENYA GOVERNMENT POLICY ON SWEET POTATO PRODUCTION AND RESEARCH PRIORITIES

Sweet potato, like other root crops such as cassava is listed as a famine reserve crop in Kenya Government documents. These include the National Development plans (1989 - 93, 94 - 96 and 97 - 2001) and Sessional Paper No (1986).

It is described as a drought-escaping crop that suits the Kenya ASALS. It has of late in the 1990's been an official policy of Kenya Government to emphasis the utilisation of ASALS, which comprise at least 75% of the total land area of the country. This in itself speaks volumes about the importance attached to sweet potatoes.

However there seems to be a contradiction in the government's approach to implementing the policies. KARI, the main government agricultural research body, rates sweet potato 37th out of 52 crops on research prioritization. This was in a 1990 - 2000 crops research prioritization in Kenya. Again, unlike other temperate crops, KARI has no formal research station for sweet potatoes (at least up to 1997). The fact that sweet potato is described as a subsistence crop with good production potentials means that it is not given a lot of importance.

Kenya has 50 sweet potato accessions, of which 32 (64%) are local. Thus, exotic accessions are only 36%, rendering East Africa a probable centre of origin of sweet potato besides the tropical America. Thus, there seems to be a lot of indigenous/folk knowledge of agronomic and processing packages of the crop. Thus, the existing yield gap 2.5T and 50T per hectare means that there is a lot in stock for agricultural extentionists. The yield component can be improved while also attending to the previously stated production hindrances. Since many traditional farmers seem to have internalised the cultivation and use of this crop, they should be involved in a collaborative research. This should aim at maximizing yields while increasing chemical quality, organoleptic acceptability, industrial use and processing techniques. Drought, pest and disease resistance, coupled with long shelf life, should be top in the sweet potato research.

It is due to some of the stated problems and poor attention by researchers that the yields and production in Africa remain low. The 1996 target of 556,220 tons has never been achieved to date. The 1992 production was 504,220 tons has against a target of over 550,00 tons.

Table 11 : Sweet Potato Production in Kenya

Year	1982	1970	1960
National Production tons (Kenya)	350,000	460,000	450,000
Global production (x 1,000 t)	140,186	94,000	111,000

5.14 CONCLUSIONS AND RECOMMENDATIONS

Farmers in their own dryland eco-zones have devised means of coping with the planting material problem. For those who immediately neighbour the lake, many Luo Nyanza inhabitants were long used to drought. They could apportion themselves swampy lands at least each person/family having a share. Whoever was not utilising hers could be requested to release it to somebody else.

These farmers, normally women, could cultivate sweet potatoes on parts of their plots - near or away from the waters depending on the season. As a dry season approached, they could move progressively towards the lake. As rains approached, they slowly moved away from the lake so that they avoided the flooding commonly associated with the swamps. When the potatoes near the lake were flooded, brave people could brave the waters to go and uproot some of the tubers lest it all got lost, swallowed up and rotted in the waters.

The swamps should therefore be utilized only for environmentally friendly crops to ensure they effectively play their roles as buffer zones. Potato varieties are known in their tens many of which remain a preserve of the local traditional producers of the crop. There is thus a need for collaborative research and production package development for this crop. The collaborators should be outsiders (i.e development agent residing temporarily in the community for reasons of imparting positive agricultural changes), local elites (members of the community who are recognized on their capacity in different respect), and the real community. The community should be viewed as comprising experienced personnel with vast knowledge of the agricultural history, food (in)security calendars, past adoption records and all edaphic economic, agronomic, social, spiritual, cultural, political, environmental and ecological of their locality.

An appropriate research institution (local and otherwise) and end user (farmer) link should be established, taking into account the farmers priorities and problems however capital resource endowed it is. A new version of agriculture, sustainable agriculture, needs to address resource mobilization at all levels to address real needs.

CHAPTER SIX : *Manihot esculentum:* CASSAVA - Manioc - tapioca

6.00 Historical background: Origin and Domestication

Cassava, otherwise known as Tapioca or manioc, is believed to have originated in North Eastern Brazil. However the centre of diversity is Latin America east of the Andes Mountains. It was the third crop developed by the ancient American farmers. Another possible centre of origin is Central America.

6.02 SPREAD

The European exploration and expedition of the 13th Century helped in the introduction of the crop to Africa. This was reinforced by long periods of European settlement in the Tropical Africa in the 16th and 17th centuries. In the 16th Century, new world crops including cassava had reached West Africa. Like other root crops, it is believed to have evolved between the tropical forest and savanna zones of West Africa from where it was taken by the Portuguese to East Africa. Since the introduction, it has been virtually a peasant crop in the dryland.

The most recent development in the dispersal of tropical crops has been associated with expansion of tropical research in the tropics coupled with international cooperation, which has included the exchange of seeds. This effort culminated in the establishment of IBPGR (International Board for Plant Genetic Resources) in 1970's. This collects, conserves and disperses plant genetic resources on global cases. This, however, conserves a negligible proportion of genetic resources since it is too urban - biased and urban - based.

6.03 GROWTH HABITS AND IMPORTANCE OF CASSAVA

Cassava is a famine reserve crop in many parts of the tropical world. It stores food in swollen underground structures whose yield is often thrice that of cereals. The starchy roots provide more food energy per unit land than any other known root crop. It provides 8.2 million calories per hectare, the second highest among all known food crops. It is second to sugarcane in productivity. It is only followed by sweet potatoes, which provide 7.4 million calories per hectare.

The roots/tubers can normally store in the soil for as long as they are not immediately required for use. Thus even when mature, the crop can be left to stay in the field to await needy famine seasons. It is due to these that it is called a famine reserve crop. Since famine is more prevalent in drier environments, where Cassava also best performs, it even serves the purpose of famine reserve better.

These qualities render cassava the most widely grown root crop globally and are one of the most dominant food crops of Africa especially in West and Central Africa. Since the tubers grow deep into the soil, it helps remove leached nutrients from those deeper soil zones. Thus it is an important nutrient recycling crop worth considering in a crop rotation cycle. The leaves of cassava are also a rich source of vitamins and minerals when utilized as a vegetable. It is a delicacy among many communities in

Africa and Asia.

6.04 ECOLOGICAL REQUIREMENTS

Cassava is a dryland crop capable of performing impressively even in highly impoverished soils. It is very drought resistant, rendering it a marginal and small-scale crop. Cassava best does at altitudes below 1500m above sea level. It requires about 1050 - 1500 mm of precipitation in very hot environments for maximum yield. However it is a drought resistant and does reasonably well even with 500 - 800 mm pa. It only needs good rains to establish. The temperature where manioc best performs is 25 - 29^0 C. Going by these climatic requirements, cassava is a typical tropical crop. It best performs in sunny weather in the tropical regions lying between 15^{0}N and 15^{0}S of the equator. It is very popular in the lake Victoria basin.

As far as edaphic conditions are concerned, tapioca requires light soils. They can be either sandy, sandy clay or sandy loam. Very compact soils of pure clay suppress tuber formation and development. Clay soils are also susceptible to water logging due to poor drainage, a condition to which cassava responds very negatively. It needs soft, pliable, well-drained soils of medium fertility. Soils that are fertile or generally have a lot of nitrogen are inappropriate for cassava production. High amounts of nitrogen tend to increase shoot growth at the expense of tuber growth resulting in low yields. Besides high nitrogen in the soil increases the concentration of prussic acid in both the leaves and the tubers. The nutritional significance of prussic acid will be discussed later.

The main component of the crop normally utilized almost universally wherever cassava is cultivated are the tubers. These are products of secondary thickening of the previously laid down fibrous roots. Thus tuberisation is an increase in the girth of a root. It is affected by day length, rendering it a photoperiodic phenomenon. Under short day conditions, tuberization occurs readily. The process is delayed and low yields result when days lengths exceed 10 - 12 hours.

6.05 AGRONOMIC REQUIREMENTS OF TAPIOCA

The crop is propagated vegetatively by use of stem cuttings. Once a field is well prepared, free from weeds either ridges or holes are dug. Ridges are necessary where there is frequent water logging and/or soils are relatively shallow. Holes 40 - 50 cm long and slanting (i.e. deeper at one end than the other) are made uniformly 50 cm - 1 m apart.

Cuttings from mature stems are cut each 30 - 45 cm long. They should have at least 4 node points with root and shoot initials. They are planted at the onset of rains at a slanting angle of at most 45°. The stem is then half buried by the soil. With right conditions, the cuttings soon develop roots and shoots within 1 -2 weeks. Water logging at this stage normally gives a very poor start, with roots only poorly developed. At worst, it causes rotting of the cuttings. This is why choice of land is important in successful establishment of cassava.

Response to fertilizers is said to be poor. However, positive contribution of Phosphatic fertilizers should be expected since this ensures proper and elaborate root establishment. It is only that formal researchers have never seen the need of applying inorganic fertilizers to cassava fields, one of the African crops openly neglected. The negative effects of nitrogenous fertilizers look possible and convincing. The prussic acid content on the tubers is proportional to soil nitrogen content and inversely proportional to soil potassium content.

The roots develop much earlier in the life of the crop. Tuberization follows later with the established roots enlarging. Tubers normally even force their way through rocks thus acquiring differently distorted shapes. Otherwise the normal shape of a cassava tuber is either spherical or cylindrical. Obviously, water logging renders useless the role of roots, resulting in their poor development. Thus where waterlogging is likely, proper drainage should be ensured.

It takes six to nine months for a cassava crop to be ready. Thus early weeding is essential to ensure proper shoot growth and utilization of available nutrients. Weeds intensify competition for light, minerals and water. Thus early weeding ensures that both the shoot and the root have no competition. In root crops, it is believed that with proper soil conditions, shoot biomass is directly proportional to tuber yield.

The weeding aspect remains controversial in many tropical African countries. Many traditional cassava producing and consuming communities believe that weeding does not affect yield as long as the crop is cultivated as a famine reserve crop. It is not uncommon to come by heavily weed infested cassava fields in many rural environments. Such crops when given enough time to mature, normally to the tune of 1 year, produce handsomely. An old mother in Kasau village of Bondo District, Kenya had this experience.

"My husband has 12 heads of cattle to take care of.. You know, these days he tethers them. He used to lightly graze the animals in that lower field. However in April last year, I planted cassava in that lower field so he started bringing the cattle to my other weed infested paddock that still had some mature cassava. Both the goats and even the cattle were left free to graze here, untethered. Within no time, they had eaten up all the shoots of the crop. I abandoned the field. The livestock used that plot for eight good months. They left it for dead. I did not bother about the field again. However when the rains came this year, some cassava plants started coming up from that wasted overgrazed plot. Out of curiosity I went to dig wherever these young plants were sprouting. To my dismay from one site I harvested 10 tubers, each the size of the head of a mature human being."

Weeding of cassava thus looks only advantageous from the ease of harvesting point of view. From yield point of view, it may play an insignificant role as long as the crop is left long enough to mature.

6.06 POSSIBLE REASONS FOR WEED RESISTANCE BY CASSAVA

Cassava seems to be weed resistant. Weeds intensify competition for water and minerals from the soil. Thus for a plant to out - compete others in such a competitive environment, it must produce a very elaborate root system. Thus weeds intensify cassava root development which enables it to effectively absorb sufficient nutrients and water even in relatively marginal environments.

If the soils are infertile, this is even more to the advantage of cassava at the expense of its competitors. This is so because cassava does well even in soils deemed too poor for other crops. The latter will show deficiency symptoms, the most common and immediate of which are stunting and chlorosis. With reduced photosynthetic efficiency and growth rate, cassava readily smothers the weeds. It is thus healthy even in relatively unhealthy soils. The physiological and biochemical explanations remain a mystery. However, the crop has an obvious advantage over others (weeds included) in relatively poor soils.

Once it smothers the weeds with well-established root system, the roots soon start undergoing secondary thickening (i.e. tuberization). It tuberises by actively utilising any rains to photosynthesis and storing the photosynthates in the well-established sinks, the roots. It thus utilizes the competition - free environment to maximize productivity and translocation. The roots thus enlarge uninhibited.

It looks clear that as far as yields are concerned, weeding of cassava plays minimum, if any, role. However from management point of view, weeding is as important as any other operation. However, it should be done very early before active root establishment and enlargement sets in. Should late weeding of a cassava field be necessary, it should be very light and shallow. It should be accomplished by simply slashing. Alternatively a cover crop such as cowpeas or beans can be planted in a cassava field as an under crop. These can effectively smother weeds.

Late deep weeding in cassava fields account for at least 10% of yield reduction. This is because there are risks of cutting, bruising and creating wounds on established tubers. When thus treated, the tubers rot or become watery. The wounds also become entries for secondary infections, thereby resulting in a disease infected crop.

6.07 HARVESTING AND YIELD

Depending on variety and ecological conditions, the crop matures in 4 - 9 months. When mature, cracks are often seen on the soil surface overlying the tubers.

Harvesting can be done with either the entire plant removed or individual tubers harvested. Individual tubers can be located from the positions of the soil cracks from where they are dug out. Therefore if only a few tubers are to be harvested, even a crop with only a few soil cracks around its roots can be harvested from. However, if the whole crop is to be uprooted it is better only plants with at least 3 large soil cracks are uprooted. This is because it can be assumed that the plant has had most of its roots fully developed into tubers. The ones with a few cracks most likely still have many underdeveloped tubers. Thus uprooting everything at that stage substantially compromises the potential yield of the crop and the whole field.

It is therefore important to keep a cassava field clean to ensure efficient harvesting. Soft, well-pulverized soils tremendously ease harvesting since the whole crop can be pulled out with minimum, if any, loses. Almost all tubers come out attached to the stem cutting from which they developed. Then they can be individually removed.

Whereas this method saves time, labour and produce, it is only possible in humid environments where soils are also moist most of the time. It happens that cassava is not a crop for which medium and high potential environments are spared. It is largely a dryland crop. Thus the use of hand tools and equipment such as jembes and hoes in cassava harvesting is very common.

In many traditional rural settings, a field in which cassava is established is permanently a cassava field. This is because any single cassava plant harvested normally sees a new cutting planted at the exact spot from where the old crop has been uprooted. A stage thus reaches when in a single field, cassava at different growth and maturity stages all exist. The field is only regularly slashed, or lightly cultivated for an under crop to be established. Occasionally, it is burnt when it is too bushy.

6.08 YIELD

Cassava yields are as varied as the number of communities cultivating it, agro-ecological zones, varieties, prevailing food situation and cropping system.

The inhabitants of Kambe and Ribe locations of Kilifi District, Kenya, plant the stem cuttings vertically. Thus the resulting yields are very low with only one large tuber from a single plant. The Luo of Homabay district have several cassava varieties, each with a distinct use for which it is produced. The Luo of Siaya district on the other hand have very few types and varieties of cassava. Thus the cassava cultivated in this area serves all purposes - boiling, grinding etc. Thus harvesting is often done even when crops are not mature due to the many competing uses. Again the cooking types of cassava yield much less than the processing types.

Similarly, in marginal areas such as Siaya, Bondo and Kitui districts famine is a very common occurrence. Therefore cassava is at times harvested long before maturity. This also happens in areas with many cassava thieves. These strike a field and harvest everything at night when there are any signs of mature crops. Whatever the production and harvesting circumstances, cassava yields are never a disappointment. It ranges between 2.5 and 25 tons/ha. In 1974, global and Africa's cassava yields were 9t/ha and 7.2 t/ha respectively.

Root tubers have a relatively high harvesting index. This is the proportion of the biomass that is edible. They have 70% while cereals have between 20% and 60%. Thus not any photosynthetic time of a root crop is wasted; all is converted into edible matter. Cassava alone provides 8.2 million calories/ha, the second highest among all crops. It is second to sugarcane, a known C_4 plant.

6.09 CHEMICAL COMPOSITION OF CASSAVA LEAVES AND TUBER

Both tubers and leaves of cassava are utilized as food. The cassava peel comprises 10 - 20% of the entire tuber yield. The cork layers on the other hand, comprise 0.5 - 2% of the total tuber weight. The edible fleshy portion is 80 - 90% with 20 - 25% starch. It has 2% digestible crude protein content and a gross crude protein level of 3.5%.

⇒ Leaves are rich in vitamin C (35 mg/100g);

⇒ The tuber is rich in Arginine but low in methionine, Phenylalanine, tyrosine, lysine and Tryptophan. These are amino acids.

⇒ Has 35g crude protein/kg fresh matter of tuber.

⇒ Contains 5.29 mg/kg total oxalate

⇒ Has 63% moisture content and provides 12.8 mJ /kg DM

⇒ Has prussic acid content of

    a) 10 -490 mg/kg in fresh tuber depending on variety

    b) 200 mg/kg in fresh leaves

⇒ Because it belongs to the Euphorbiaceae family, it contains laticifers, thus produces latex. This white fluid comes out of tuber peels, leaves or stems. This chemical reinforces its drought resistance and heat tolerance.

6.10 NUTRITIONAL SIGNIFICANCE OF PRUSSIC ACID IN CASSAVA

Cassava contains 2 major cyanogenic glucoside, linamarin and lotaustralin. The former is synthesized from Valine, an amino acid, while the latter is synthesized from Isoleucine. Both are highly water-soluble and decompose when heated to temperatures exceeding 150°C. Under the influence of an enzyme, linamarase (linase), also present in the cassava plant, both glucosides are broken down to prussic (Hydrocyanic) acid - in the intact plant.

Relationship with Protein Synthesis and relative concentrations:

The prussic acid produced by the hydrolysis may be used as a building block for the amino acid, asparagine. The concentration of prussic acid range between 10 and 490 mg/kg of tuber. The leaves, however, have a concentration of 200 mg/kg of fresh leaves. Leaves tend to contain more of the glucosides than tubers. The leaves also contain at least 100 times more linase than the tubers. Therefore there is a tendency for more prussic acid to be in leaves than in tubers. If 0.1 mg of the glucoside is taken in one meal, it is lethal.

The concentration of prussic acid tends to vary with the level of soil fertility and the soil moisture content. Cassava growing in soils low in potassium or high in nitrogen has more prussic acid. Similarly, cassava grown in wet/moist regions has higher prussic acid than those in drier ecozones. Thus prussic acid concentration increases with moisture content of tubers. It is for this reason that cassava harvested in dry season is sweet, while the same cassava becomes bitter when harvested in wet season. In the Luo Nyanza, cassava tends to be sweet from September to April, while they tend to be bitter between May and August. The bitter taste in cassava is imparted by prussic acid.

Physiological effects of Prussic Acid, and its

detoxication:

Prussic acid/hydrocyanic acid (HCN) is a respiratory poison. Coupled with the bitter taste it imparts into foods, most cassava processing techniques aim at reducing its concentration. It is also on basis of prussic acid concentration that some cassava are eaten fresh or after boiling, while others are only used after thorough drying. In South Nyanza, there is clear demarcation among varieties either used as food directly or thoroughly processed prior to use.

Whereas a stranger would not dare feed on a cassava meal, those used to producing and utilising cassava in their homes even know what varieties and which part of cassava to eat raw. They know that 'selele' variety is the sweetest in both raw and boiled form since it has least prussic acid content. Even for those with relatively higher acid content, the rural folks know that the peel and the outermost layer of the peeled tuber have most of the acid. Thus they peel, and then scrape the outermost layer before eating such tubers raw. Otherwise one has stomach upsets and some temporary restlessness. This is common village knowledge. Boiling and drying is sufficient treatment, however.

6.11 VARIETIES AND KINDS OF CASSAVA

Traditional cassava producing and utilising communities know the varieties for eating and those for processing. The processing types are those that have to be chopped, dried and ground before use. The eating types, on the other hand, are used in their fresh form, raw or roasted.

The processing type of tapioca tends to be bitter, seemingly because of high prussic acid content, with relatively higher yields. One plant can yield 50 - 100 t/ha. Some also grow into tall shrubs of even 4 - 5m. The eating type however tend to be sweeter, lower yielding, and between 1 - 2 m tall. Among known varieties are:

⇒ Nyandhaga (Cannabis Sativa (Njaga) like in leaf structure)

⇒ Otuga (otugo diep)

⇒ Nyauganda

⇒ Kamisi

⇒ Selele - sweet type; tubers whitish in their coat, lower yields.

6.12 Processing and use of Cassava

There are numerous processing and cooking techniques of cassava. Each method depends on the intended use of the product. The fresh tuber has moisture content of up to 60%. This renders it perishable once harvested, as it becomes very prone to fungal attack. Many processing techniques therefore strive to either reduce the moisture content and/or the prussic acid content.

a) Boiled Cassava   Since prussic acid is not thermo-stable, it is greatly broken down by boiling. At a temperature of 73^0 C, the concentration of prussic acid in cassava tubers greatly reduce to non - lethal levels. The better if the tuber is boiled at this temperature until it becomes soft. Thus whatever the variety of cassava, boiling renders it safe for direct consumption. This is what will be referred to thereafter as boiled cassava. Prior to heat treatment, the fresh tuber is peeled, halved, the pith removed and divided into convenient sizes to enhance cooking. Smaller pieces cook faster.

b) Chips Alternatively the cooking cassava can be peeled, halved, de-pithed and broken into finger like pieces called chips. These are washed, salted, left to rest for some minutes, then either deep-fried or half boiled before being deep-fried. This produces chips.

c) Crisps A third method of processing the cooking cassava is the making of crisps. Once the tuber is peeled halved and de-pithed, thin paper like platy pieces are sliced out, dried and deep-fried. The result, called crisps, is very common in coastal towns in Kenya.

d) Marsh A fourth form of processing of the eating cassava is done like this. After the obvious first three stages of processing, the tuber is sliced into conveniently small pieces, boiled thoroughly then cooked. This produces a mash.

e) Roast The eating cassava can also be roasted and eaten as a roast. This is common among the Luo, but is an adored processing method among the Marakwet, a sub tribe of the kalenjin of Rift Valley of Kenya. The producers of this crop hail from the drier, hotter Kerio Valley - areas such as Tot and Aror. They simply roast the cassava and take them even to far markets such as Kapsowar, Cheptongei or Chebiemit for sale.

f) Cassava Flour For the processing type of cassava, there is relatively higher prussic acid content besides the tubers being much larger. Therefore it undergoes similar processing pathways such as peeling, halving, chopping, drying and grinding. Before chopping, de-pithing can either be done or omitted depending on the community in question.

> The resulting flour is normally very fine, with some sticky wheat like qualities when moistened. The flour can be used for making any form of gruel alone or mixed with one of the following, sorghum, millet, maize and sweet potato flour. Cassava can also be used in the industry to produce starch. Starch is used as a filler material or as a laboratory chemical.

6.13 Uses of Processed Cassava.

The boiled cassava makes a good cassava meal. The chips are popular, very fast replacing the traditionally known Irish potato chips in many urban kiosks. Crisps are popular snacks in Coast province towns as well as main upcountry hotels as part of either snack or breakfast. The roast remains largely a home - based technique except among the Marakwet who take it to the public markets for sale. The flour can be used to make any form of gruel thick or thin (i.e. porridge or Ugali). It is also used in some ratio with wheat and/or sorghum, millet flour for baking.

For the leaves, they are rich source of vitamins and minerals when prepared as vegetables. However, first the prussic acid content has to be reduced to a convenient and safe level. This is done by first sun drying, then chopping or crushing and boiling the leaves for a few minutes. The resulting water is discarded as it contains the bulk of the acid. The resulting leaves are cooked in the normal way any vegetable is treated such as frying. It makes a cheap nourishing meal.

After elucidating these important aspects of cassava, it is important at this stage to discuss the spatial (local and global) production and utilisation.

6.14 PRODUCTION OF CASSAVA

Siaya district, one of the typical cassava zones in Kenya produced 6,915.20 tons in 4322 hectares, in 1993 this boils down to 1.600 t/ha.

Table 12: Kenya and Global Production statistics for cassava (1960,70 and 82)

Year	1960	1970	1982
Kenya	500,000	620,000	650,000
Global	73,500,000	96,600,000	128,000,000

CHAPTER SEVEN: OIL CROPS: SIMSIM AND GROUNDNUTS

7.00 SIMSIM (*Sesamum indicum*)   Sesame

7.01 Background

Simsim is a wild plant in Africa. Better varieties seem to have been grown by African farmers for a very long time before its spread to Asia. It certainly seems to be a very old farm crop in Africa because of the ceremonies used for ensuring good yields in which it was involved. In Botswana, there are some wild varieties of Simsim, depicting it as a pure dryland crop.

Use of Simsim in cultural activities including songs was common. In an Acoli traditional poem, translated by Okot P' Bitek, line 4 reads: " Her teeth are white like dry season Simsim". This statement tells a lot about the African knowledge and use of Simsim. In Arthur Thomas's book (1967) entitled Farming in Hot climates, it is stated that in one African country the seed would not germinate in one experimental plot until some old ladies of the country were asked to grow it.

> Any attempt to understand the poor and learn from them, has to begin with introspection by the outsiders themselves. We have first to examine ourselves and identify and offset our preconceptions, prejudices and rationalizations. (Chambers, 1983)

Certainly, Africa seems to be the centre of origin (diversity) and domestication of Simsim. The knowledge of its production processing and use remains a preserve of Africans.

7.02   ECONOMIC IMPORTANCE

Simsim is an oil, proteinous crop traditionally grown in Africa for many cultural uses. It is grown for confectionery purposes. It is one of the richest oilseeds known, with a concentration of 45%. The protein content is also very high being 20% and 1.5 % Calcium. Thus in terms of proteins, energy and minerals it rates very highly. It is of great industrial potential for extraction of oil.

Considering the dangerous levels of Protein Energy Malnutrition (PEM) and desertification in sub - Saharan Africa, Simsim can be a very important compromise crop. It is drought resistant and drought escaping due to a short maturing period, and a good source of essential fatty acids. It can give sesame cakes and oils thereby acting as a source of food and feed. Like its groundnut counterpart Simsim provides essential fatty acids such as linoleic, linolenic, arachidoic and arachidonic acids. Coupled with the high energy density, it is a crop worth producing in bulk.

7.03   ECOLOGICAL REQUIREMENTS

Simsim is an extremely drought resistant crop. It needs 400 mm pa during the growing season, though it grows best with 750 mm pa. It requires warm climates of temperatures at least 20 C. This is most common in attitudes less than 1500 m ASL. It is intolerant to water logging. Due to the attitude and temperatures requirements, Simsim best does in Coast and Nyanza provinces and to some extent Western province of Kenya.

Simsim can do reasonably well even in impoverished soils. This advantage, coupled with drought resistance and short maturity period, makes it a crop of the semi-arid parts of Kenya, which is at least 75% of the total area. Since aridity is fast catching up even with the hitherto moist environments, it is a crop of the future.

7.04 AGRONOMIC REQUIREMENTS

The seeds of Simsim are very tiny. This requires that the seedbed meant for the crop be very fine. However, when it is extremely fine, winds tend to blow away many seeds leading to losses. In addition, the seeds become prone to pests, as it is a delicacy to many kinds of birds.

Therefore, a relatively rough seedbed is needed. Care needs to be taken to ensure that the tilth is not too rough as the clods tend to cover many seeds. This leads to lots of losses as well as seedling abortion. This results when the seed gets the right germination conditions but due to excess soil cover fails to emerge. The failure to emerge arises from exhaustion of the stored nutrients, which at some stage needs to be supplemented with photosynthates. If the soil/clod cover exceeds the penetrating power of the seedling, no light reaches the seedling resulting in its abortion/death. Therefore a rough seedbed of moderate tilth is needed.

The crop, with very small seeds, is hard to sow by hill placement. Therefore broadcasting is the most common and indeed the oldest sowing method. The seed size has made the mechanizations of sesame production hard. It is therefore still entirely produced manually.

The seeds are sown early in the rainy season at a rate of 5.5 - 9 kg/ha. The sowing time should be such that the crop gets 1½ - 2 months of rain, followed by a dry season for seed maturity, ripening and drying. It can be weeded twice during its production season. However it is relatively tolerant to weed infestation due to its fast growth and maturity.

7.05   HARVESTING AND YIELD

When ready, some leaves start yellowing and falling. Timing should be proper because a lot of losses can be incurred. The whole plant is uprooted or cut at the lower end with a Panga. They are then hung by tying up on a rack so that as the capsules dry up and crack, seeds may fall out. After 2 - 4 weeks, depending on the stage of harvesting, all the capsules have dried up. Some may even have started opening up. Therefore a mat has to be spread below the rack where the mature plants have been hung.

Threshing is done by beating (hitting) the hung plants with a stick, causing the capsules to break open and release their contents. These fall on the mat. Further processing involves winnowing to remove any chaff from the rest of the seeds. These are then dried and stored. If well taken care of, up to 1.5 tons of seeds per hectare can be yielded. However, the most common yield is 500 kg/ha. This is terribly low.

The low sesame yields can partly be attributed to pests and partly to the sub-optimal seed rate. The latter arises from the fact that the crop is largely produced under mixed crop system. At times the area covered by rocks and tree stumps are never considered.

7.06 STORAGE

Simsim seeds are very small and platy. Therefore they dry up very readily and store very well. Their small size is not conducive for many storage pests. Traditionally Simsim used to be kept in pit or cave. This is why in the tale of "Ali Baba and the forty thieves" the password was 'open sesame'. Sesame and Gingerly are other names of Simsim. It can also be kept in gourds and/or earthen pots.

7.07 PROCESSING

The Simsim seeds can be roasted. The result can be

(i) mixed with roasted groundnuts and sugar to make a snack called Simsim common in Bondo town and the Line Saba stage in Kibera.

(ii) finely ground/pound to make Odi. Odi is either used directly as a salad with Ugali or added to vegetables.

7.08 CHEMICAL COMPOSITION OF SESAME

This is on per 100g DM basis of edible food:

- 2400 KJ (2.4 MJ)

- 20 g proteins. The proteins are rich in Arginine, Leucine and methionine but low in lysine.

- 1500 mg calcium (15%)

- 15 mg Iron (liver has 12 mg iron per 100 g).

- 0.4 mg Thiamin

- 45 g oils

Sesame seeds are therefore important energy, protein and mineral sources and to a less extent, vitamins. These qualities make it a good crop for cottage industries for oil extraction and simple processing, as it is very rich in energy.

7.09 PRODUCTION LIMITATIONS

A number of factors hinder large scale and efficient production of sesame. These are:

i) Pests

   a) Simsim webworm (*Antigastria catalaunalis*). This affects the terminal leaves, tender shoots and pods, which are damaged. The terminal leaves are webbed together with silk, greatly retarding growth of the terminal bud. In effect, this reduces pod production and development. The caterpillars reach 13 mm long, are green bodied with black head.

b) Fleas beetles (*Aphthoria bimaculata*) eat the foliage.

ii) Diseases

a) Leaf spot - a fungal disease caused by *Cercospora sesame* and *Alternaria spp*

iii) Marketing:

There is no formal marketing institution of Simsim in Kenya and many countries. Its production therefore largely remains at subsistence level.

iv) Research:

No much research is done on Simsim productivity. The agronomic packages largely remain traditional. KARI rates Simsim in the 27th position among crops research prioritization 1990 - 2000. It is thus not considered important to the economy of the country.

8.00   GROUNDNUT (Arachis hypogea)

8.01   Origin And Historical background

Groundnuts originated in South America East of the Andes Mountains. This is the same centre of origin for cassava, cocoa, rubber and pineapple. At least 90 wild species of groundnuts exist here.

8.02   Domestication

This crop was domesticated in South America. The specific areas include South Western Brazil, Northern Argentina, Paraguay, Bolivia, Eastern Peru and the neighboring districts. Out of the 90 species, only 15 are described formally.

8.03   SPREAD

Groundnut was never known in the new world in the pre-Colombian times. It was taken from Brazil to West Africa by the Portuguese and from Peru to the Philippines by the Spanish. Since then, groundnuts spread throughout the tropics and sub tropics to latitude 40°N and 40°S of equator where rain, during the growing season, is more than 500 mm pa. In the 16th century, groundnut value was recognized by the Portuguese who introduced it into Africa. In Kenya it was introduced by the British in 1920's and 1930's. In the latter years, the colonialists were providing free seeds to Kenyan indigenous communities. Ordinary groundnut was brought from America to West Africa over 380 years ago. It is currently grown in the drier parts of most hot countries like USA, which have long hot summers. Other producers are West Africa, India, China, East

Indies and Coromandel Coast.

Fig 8: The groundnut plant.

8.04 SPATIAL DISTRIBUTION

Asia and Africa produce the bulk of the crop on global scale. In the 1970's India was producing at least 25% of the total groundnut. It is still a main producer. West Africa produces the bulk of the crop in Africa. It is the main export crop in Liberia. Nigeria's export contributions of groundnuts also rates at 20% per annum. The country produces 7% of global groundnut produce; Sudan contributes about 3% and Senegal 4%. The production in Africa has not been very steady because of quality restrictions in the importing countries in Europe. However, it is the most important Africa oil seed and form the chief crop of Senegal and Gambia.

In Kenya, production has not been steady either. Siaya district, a leading producer of the crop in 1950's, 1960's and 1970's is now a very minor producer since the crop has lost the esteem it used to be held in. Tanzania produces the bulk of East Africa's groundnuts. The annual increase in production is 20,000 tons. Nyanza and Western provinces have almost always produced the whole of Kenya's groundnuts. Table 13 below shows this.

Table 13 (a, b and c): Groundnut production in Nyanza, Western provinces and Kenya (National) Production (in tons).

d) Year	1970/71	1971/71	1972/73	1973/74	1974/75
Production in (Nyanza)(a)	3174	1960	6099	2280	2850
Production in (Western) (b)	5720	7581	8054	2845	7585
National Production in Kenya ©	8894	9541	14154	5125	10435

d	1975/76	1976/77	1977/78	1978/79	1979/80	1980/81	1981/82
a	3288	4660	2164	1965	1973	3594	1564
b	12560	29682	18207	13809	18509	9429	9919
c	15848	38052	22649	15774	20482	13023	11480

	82/83	83/84	84/85	85/86	86/87	87/88	88/89	89/90	90/91
a	2440	1924	1524	1160	2309	1740	4084	4900	4660
b	13277	1464	5787	3277	3088	4922	28634	6989	9977
c	15717	3398	7311	5437	5197	8954	22718	13260	16133

In Kenya, Siaya district was usually the leading producer, producing about 50-80% of the total Nyanza provincial production.

East Indies collectively produces the bulk of the groundnut that enters the world market. Java is most important producer and exporter. The production has been increasing since 1950's. However, market for groundnut is dwindling because of competition from soybeans, sunflower and cottonseed from the USA. Groundnut is the chief export of these island countries making 40% of export in volume. In 1982 and 1976, global production was 18.6 and 17.9 million tons respectively. The production in Kenya in 1976 was 5.5 million tons, almost representing 30% of global production. Current levels of production in Kenya are not significant.

Table 14: Groundnut production in Migori District, Kenya

MIGORI	1990	1991	1992	1992
Acreage (ha)	491	747	801	1095
Yield (90-kg bags)	13080	18680	33350	
Production (tons)	1177.20	1681.2	3001.5	87.6
Yield (tons/ha)	2.4	2.2	3.7	0.8

8.05 GROWTH HABITS

Groundnut is a warm season leguminous cover crop that takes 4 - 5 months to mature. It is relatively drought resistant with a reflective coefficient (albedo) of 0.17. It produces flowers after 2 months. Upon fertilization, the pods containing fertilized ovules bend downwards and penetrate the soil with their sharp pegged ends. This develop into mature fruits. The number of edible nuts per pod range between 1 and 6.

8.06 ECOLOGICAL REQUIREMENTS

Arachis hypogea needs good rainfall, being a warm season tropical crop of humid environments. The best amount of rainfall is 600 - 1200 mm pa, with a good amount falling during the active growing period (500 mm). It only needs 3 good months of rainfall followed by at least 3 weeks of drought to enhance crop maturity and drying. Reliable rainfall especially during flowering is important to ease pegging, a process that largely relies on softness and moistness of the soil.

Groundnut needs a warm climate throughout its growth period. Temperature requirements therefore range between 20 - 30ºC. However, the higher the temperature, the higher the transpiration losses, necessitating the availability of a lot of reliable rainfall.

Light soils are most preferred by groundnuts because this enhances pegging. This is the penetration of the soil surface by a groundnut peg. A peg is a young conical shaped pod resulting from fertilization of the ovary and with a sharp peg like tip to enhance its penetration. Heavy clay soils depress pegging and therefore maturity of fruits. Thus sandy, sandy loam or loamy soils are the best. They need to be well pulverized, well drained and fertile. Waterlogging is a hindrance to groundnut production. It depresses both the growth and pegging of the crop. Thus the need for ridges in soils of poor drainage.

8.07 AGRONOMIC REQUIREMENTS

Arachis hypogea needs a rough tilth since the seeds are large. The seedbed needs to be well prepared with both primary and secondary cultivation well done. The soil should have rested enough between secondary cultivation and planting to ensure that soil borne pests and pathogens are exposed to the harsh sunshine. This reduces their numbers. This is an important cultural method of pest and disease control.

Tertiary cultivation such as ridging is essential if the soil is prone to waterlogging. Planting is done by making holes, 10.0 cm apart on both sides of the ridges. If ridging is not necessary, holes are dug on flat land of a spacing of 15 cm x 9 cm. if mixed cropping is desired. If mono-cropping a pure stand of groundnuts is planned, then a spacing of 60 cm x 15 cm or 45 cm x 15 cm is appropriate. 2 - 3 seeds are placed in each hole, covered and the soil compacted over the planting holes. This is essential to ensure proper seed coverage by the soil as well as good contact between the soil and the seed. The seed soil contact enhances germination since the seed soon starts exerting osmotic force and therefore absorbing moisture. The erect type needs closer spacing.

The seeds germinate within 5 - 10 days. Weed control should be ensured from the earliest time possible. Up to 3 weedings are normally done in many Nyanza groundnut-producing areas. This is necessary to enforce minimum crop - weed competition and to ease harvesting. Clean field at harvesting time ensures maximum retrieval of pods, and therefore minimum crop loss. This maximizes yields.

Harvesting is done when 50% of the crops have had their foliage drying up. At this stage, a good proportion of pods of matured and very few, if any, have started detaching themselves from the mother plants. The detached pods often remain in the soil and re-grow in the following season as if another crop has been planted. Timely harvesting greatly reduces these over - maturity losses.

The whole plant is uprooted using jembes, hoes or any other implement. They are spread on the soil surface to dry up for 2 - 3 days. This is why it is recommended that harvesting be done during the dry sunny months. Then individual pods are plucked, further dried, shelled and the seeds stored. The yield depends on variety and management, and averages 1 ton/ha.

8.08 POST HARVEST PROCESSING, STORAGE AND USES.

Once the nuts are removed from the pods, they are dried to moisture content of 12 - 15 %. It takes a long time to fully dry up the nuts because of the high oil content. However, dry seeds store better and for a long time. The nuts can be put to any of the following processing procedures:

1) Roasting: The nuts are sorted, moistened put in a heating pan and regularly stirred (mixed). When patches of the nuts have turned dark, they are ready. This is the roasted groundnut.

2) Pound Ground Nut: The nuts are first roasted before being pound by a pestle and mortar. It

acquires pasty foam as the peanut butter. This is the pound ground nut or peanut butter.

3) Rough Pounding: The roasted nuts are roughly pounded, taking a rough pasty but with clodded form.

4) Groundnut Flour: The nuts are roasted and ground or milled. In grinding, the nuts are used wholly without any parts removed. In milling, the testa is first removed after roasting before being ground. The resulting powder is either rough or fine, depending on whether it is produced by grinding or milling.

8.09 USES

When processed to the different forms 1 - 4 above, each can be put to many uses. The roasted groundnut is good snack. The pounded groundnut or peanut butter is used to paste bread. It is also used for cooking many kinds of vegetables. Once a vegetable is boiled, and some water removed, the pounded groundnut paste is added as well as salt. This is a complete meal. The peanut butter is traditionally called 'Odi' by the Luo. Odi was a popular dish taken with Ugali (thick gruel) i.e. as a sauce.

Roughly pounded groundnut is traditionally used for preparing vegetable dishes. After boiling the vegetables, the pounded groundnut is added. This compensates for frying.

Groundnut flour is used to make a dish called 'Dengu'.

The flour is mixed with milk and boiled gently but thoroughly. When prepared in a cooking pot, it is very delicious. It is a popular vegetable in South Nyanza and Bondo districts, especially Uyoma.

From the industrial point of view, both oils and groundnut cakes can be extracted from the nuts. The oil contains many essential fatty acids needed by man, while the cake is popular animal concentrate feed. It is highly energy packed. The unshelled immature pods can also be boiled and eaten. Shelled, dried nuts can also be eaten raw. However, some people are allergic to the raw nuts, suffering from stomach upsets upon use. The uses depend on varieties. Different varieties have varying levels of oils, proteins and other essential fatty and amino acids. Some varieties are given below:

Manipintar (Tanzania for oil)	Homabay (confectionery)	Makulu Red (Zambia & Uganda)

8.10 STORAGE

The most important reason for keenly observing storage conditions of groundnuts is to keep them from fungal infections. This can take the form of pod or nut rotting to aflatoxin accumulation. The nutritional significance of aflatoxin is discussed later. Groundnut is an oil rich leguminous crop. It is for these two purposes - oil and protein content that it is produced. The details of chemical constitution is as follows on 100g dry matter basis:

Table 15: Chemical composition of groundnuts (per 100 g dry matter)

2.6 g proteins (i.e. 26%)	17.5 mg nicotinic acid	0.8 mg thiamine
46 g lipids (oils i.e. 46%)	0.2 g riboflavin	50 mg calcium
2.34 MJ		

The proteins have sub optimal amounts of cystine and methionine both being sulphur amino acids. The first limiting amino acid is lysine. The groundnut oils are unique in that they supply essential fatty acids such as:
(1) Linoleic $C_{17}H_{31}COOOH$, melting point - 5°C and (2) Arachidonic acids.

Other essential fatty acids that other seed-oils/oil crops provide in large quantities are arachidoic and linolenic. Groundnuts supply only a small quantity of these. In as much as groundnuts are important in supplying essential fatty acids, the acids are largely an unsaturated type that induce vitamin E deficiency/shortage if consumed in excess. Groundnut cake is a good livestock concentrate feed. However, it should not form more than 25% of the diet in pigs, as it tends to produce soft body parts and a laxative action. The latter is largely because the proportion of roughage (indigestible matter) is very low. Thus if heavily relied on, it weakens the GIT functioning.

Groundnut contents also have a growth factor and an anti-trypsin factor. Thus some individuals feel stomach upsets after feeding on groundnut meal, especially when raw. The anti-trypsin factor also has an anti-plasmin activity. Thus it shortens bleeding time (i.e. enhances blood clotting). The factor is destroyed by heating, thereby rendering roasted or cooked groundnuts safe. Those allergic to raw groundnuts should first roast them before use.

8.11   Aflatoxin:

Groundnuts also contain a poison called aflatoxin if infected by a fungus *Aflatoxin flavus*. The infection can take place in the field or in the store. Aflatoxin is classified as Aflatoxin B_1, G_1, B_2 and G_2. Of these, Aflatoxin B_1 is the most potent. It causes liver damage with marked bile duct proliferation. It also causes hepatic tumors and liver necrosis. The latter is the drying of liver cells. Aflatoxin is also a very active carcinogen.

A metabolite called Aflatoxin M has been shown to be present in milk of cows fed on toxic meals. Aflatoxin M also causes liver damage to ducklings. It is thermostable, rendering aflatoxin-infected nuts permanently toxic. Oils and fats (lipids) produce more energy than their carbohydrate counterparts do. 1 gram of carbohydrate provides 16.8 Joules while a similar quantity of lipid provides 38 Joules. This qualifies it as a high energy density food.

8.12   LIMITATIONS TO GROUNDNUT PRODUCTION

Going by the production and the yield data, it is clear that the production is dwindling. This is attributable to a number of reasons being:

a)   Pests

i) Groundnut hopper - *Hilda patruellis*: causes artificial drought symptoms. Ants attach to base of plant stems. Small brown hoping bugs up to 3 mm long in soil around roots.

ii) Systates weevil

iii) Groundnut aphid (*Aphis crassivora*) is a vector of the groundnut rosette virus, which distorts plant leaves.

iv) Bark eating termites - *Macrotermes spp*. Feeds on the shells of the nuts, making them rough. They weaken the shells so that they easily release the nuts, which easily germinate. They also detach the pods from the mother plant, thereby resulting in a lot of nut loses. The wet wood termite *Coptotermes formosanus*, also causes similar damage.

v) Cotton bud thrips: *Frankliniella schulzei* distorts the leaves of groundnuts thus reducing photosynthetic surface area and area exposed to the sun.

vi) Bean flower thrips: *Taeniothrips sjostedti* affects the flowers of groundnuts, seriously reducing yield.

b) Diseases

i) Aflatoxin flavus: infects the developing nuts inside pods. Produces a toxin, aflatoxin, that is carcinogenic and a potent poison. The fungus-based toxin is encouraged by moist conditions.

ii) Groundnut Rosette virus (GRV): GRV is transmitted by a pest *Aphis crassivora* and distorts plant leaves. This greatly reduces photosynthetic surface area and the yield.

iii) Leaf Spot Blight - caused by a fungus, *Sclerotium rolfsi*

c) Marketing:

There are no formalized marketing institutions of groundnuts in Kenya. Many farmers largely produce for subsistence because of poor market channels. The industries that could consume the product such as cooking oil and soap industries prefer to import from other countries their raw materials. Thus to date, oil seed imports constitute a large proportion of total annual imports of Kenya. Table 16 below shows some import data.

About KShs 1.2 billion is spent every year to accomplish the edible oilseed imports coupled with an import of oilseed cake costing a further 1.1 billion per annum. Thus over 2.3 billion Kshs is used annually in imports. This is a loss and could be used to boost oilseed production in Kenya. By 1988, United States was the largest edible Oilseed producer, topping 52 million tons. China, Brazil, India and Argentina followed.

Table 16: The 1986 - 94 vegetable oil and fat imports to Kenya: (in tons)

1994	1986	1987	1988	1989	1990	1991	1992	1993
296235	101724	125835	125427	-	160875	174676	189974	138505

With an annual consumption growth rate of 13% between 1978 and 1992 for edible oils, the imports have continued increasing. The annual national requirements are 220,000 tons currently (1999/2000).

d) Poor prioritization of national research needs Kenya's main research organ rates groundnuts a poor 20th out of 52 crops in order of research prioritization. The potential consumer industries of this important edible oilseed crop are also not involved in any research or production.

8.13 RESEARCH NEEDS FOR GROUNDNUTS

The immediate research needs of groundnuts include:

a) Breeding for high yields and high methionine, cystine and cysteine amino acid - these being sulphur -based essential amino acids.

b) Breeding for *Aflatoxin flavus* resistant varieties

c) Breeding for reduced ant-nutritional factors such as anti-trypsin factor.

d) Increased drought resistance since many varieties need a minimum of 600 mm pa during active growing season. This condition puts off many otherwise climatically suitable areas in Kenya thereby lowering production.

8.14 OIL CROPS, PULSE CROPS AND THEIR PRODUCTION NEEDS

The current annual national requirements of oilseed in Kenya are 200,000 tons. Of this at least 95% is imported every year. The imports cost about Ksh 2.4 billion with Ksh 1.2 billion spent on actual edible oilseed and a further Ksh 1.2 billion on oilseed meal.

The consumption of edible oils grew at a about 13% per annum between 1978 and 1992 in Kenya. The turnover of the oilseed subsection is estimated to be around Ksh 12 billion. With a population growth of 3.8% pa in Kenya and a low per capita consumption of 5.6 kg, the country will require 250,000 tons of vegetable oil and 80,000 tons of protein meal by the year 2000. Fats release 9.3 K calories/g compared with carbohydrates, which release 3.8 Kcal/g.

Currently the average annual per capita consumption of edible oilseed in developing countries is 7kg, while that for the developed countries is 24 kg. Despite this low consumption level in oilseeds, the ministry of Agriculture records show a steady decline in oilseed production since 1980's. The highest acreage and yields was realized in 1987 with 113,000 ha and 70,000 t of oilseed released. This scenario is discouraging. Many African countries, Kenya included spend a lot of resources in the name of foreign exchange to import many commodities that could otherwise be better produced internally. Among notable oilseed crops with high potential in dryland regions are sunflower, Simsim, soybeans, coconuts, groundnuts, cashew nuts and castor oil plant. As long as policy emphasis is not directed towards these hidden resources, the import bill on edible oils is bound to be a heavy burden to the economy. Dependence on importation, in any case, significantly reduces the production of these crops, which are rendered market-less.

CHAPTER NINE: PULSE CROPS

9.0 Cowpeas: (*Vigna unguiculata*)

9.01 Historical Background

Cowpea has its centre of origin in Ethiopian region, the same centre of origin of a wide range of tropical African crops. However, its wild forms are widely distributed in Africa.

Vigna is a tropical group of plants, a genus of about 170 species. It has the largest number of species endemic to Africa. Only 4 species, *V. unguiculata, V. radiata* and *V. sinensis* and *V. mungo* are economically important.

9.02 Domestication:

Cowpea was first domesticated in Ethiopian region. Others also think that the crop was domesticated in West Africa, or perhaps widely throughout the African savannah zone, more than 4000 years ago (i.e. before 2000BC). It is thought to have evolved together with millets and sorghum with which it has, since time immemorial, been intercropped. The wild forms of *Vigna unguiculata* occur only in Africa.

9.03 SPREAD

Cowpea was introduced to America from Africa during the slave trade and given the name cowpea. This is because it was a popular plant for livestock (cow) feed. The earliest cultivars of cowpeas in Africa were the spreading, photosensitive, short day types of subspecies *unguiculata*. Cowpea probably reached India together with millet and sorghum from East Africa around 1500 BC.

9.04 IMPORTANCE OF COWPEAS:

The crop is widely cultivated for their leaves and pods which produce pulse. It is rich in even the often-deficient sulphur amino acids such as cystine and methionine, among others. It contains reasonably high concentrations of minerals such as iron and calcium. Besides, it is so rich in vitamins such as B_2 (Riboflavin) and B_1 (Thiamine). The leaves are rich in vitamin A. It also supplies a reasonably impressive energy quantity.

Cowpea is a pulse crop with the highest potential of all food legumes in the semi and sub humid tropical lowlands. It has the advantages of quick, early growth, short maturity, wide ecological adaptation, drought resistance, grain quality, acceptability, broad range of genetic diversity and ease of hybridization. If production can be promoted, it can greatly help reduce the food insecurity inherent in the dryland South.

9.05 ECOLOGICAL REQUIREMENTS

Cowpea is warm climate lowland crop of the tropics. It requires an annual precipitation of 800 mm pa. However, even with 400 - 500 mm pa well distributed over the growing season, it performs modestly.

The best temperature for cowpea is anything above 18°C. For this it does best in lowland areas of altitude less than 1500 m above sea level. However, if cultivated for leaf production, it does well in much higher altitude, even 3000m. The low temperatures associated with high altitudes greatly suppress pod production and development. Therefore if cultivated as a pulse crop, it should be restricted to areas below 1500m ASL.

Cowpea is a leguminous crop that can fix atmospheric nitrogen. Thus it does not need very fertile soils if meant for pulse. However, if meant for leaf production, it needs a reasonably fertile soil. The soils need to be of good drainage not prone to waterlogging. The crop thus needs an agro-ecological zone of lower midlands 4 - 5 or lowlands 3 - 4. The upright determinate cultivars of the cylindrical subspecies are more drought resistant than their unguiculata counterparts.

9.06 AGRONOMIC REQUIREMENTS

Cowpea evolved together with millet and sorghum in the dryland Africa. Its production requirements are therefore known best by these traditional farmers. In the traditional cereal farming system of West Africa, the spreading, short - day cowpeas were inter-planted with sorghum or pearl millet about six weeks after the cereals were sown in a well prepared land. Broadcasting was the most popular planting method. Up to 20kg of seed was needed per hectare as planting material. However, where only foliage is required seeds were broadcasted at the rate of 100 kg ha^{-1}.

Modern agriculture has come up with single/pure stand or monoculture cropping systems that have been applied to almost all crops. Under such circumstances, seeds are sown directly at a rate of 66 kg seed/ha, and with a spacing of 75 cm x 5 - 8 cm. The seeds are placed 4 inches deep. Early weeding is advocated for since the crop provides almost full soil cover within 4 weeks. At that stage, they completely smother any other under-growth. This is why traditionally they were sown at least a month after the cereal crops.

If the crop is meant for seed/pod production, the terminal bud is pruned after 2 - 3 weeks of sowing. This encourages the growth of lateral buds from where most pods later develop. If topping is not done, the fields become too bushy with a lot of leafy growth. The pruned terminal buds are used as vegetables.

If produced for leaf, harvesting begins from the third week. Harvesting can then be done on a regular basis, the duration depending on the extent of each. However, one week is a fair enough time lapse between leaf harvestings.

9.07 HARVESTING AND YIELD

Leaf harvesting begins from the third week of sowing. This can continue for even 4 months depending on the prevailing ecological conditions. Up to 2 tons can be harvested from a field set entirely for leaf production. In the traditional African farming system, cowpea was cultivated both for leaves and pod (seed) yields. In such circumstances, an extrapolated seed and leaf yields could be 750 Kg and 1 ton respectively.

In some farming systems cowpea is produced purposely for seed yield. The yield depends on the variety. Thus the more heat and drought tolerant cylindrical subspecies yield much higher than their unguiculata counterparts do. Seed yield from an entirely pod purpose single stand of cowpeas yield between 500 kg ha $^{-1}$ and 6 t/ha. The latter has been achieved in humid research stations. The former is assumed to have been recorded from a traditional mixed crop and multi purpose cowpea field, with clearly significant under-use of the land.

In Kenya, Migori district records 2 t/ha. There is no corresponding national yield. Seeds can yield 1.5 t/ha within 70 days of sowing and 3 t/ha within 95 days. Harvesting of seeds continues for 4 - 5 months.

9.08   CHEMICAL COMPOSITION

Both leaves and pods are utilized as food. They have the following based on 100 g dry matter:

- ⇒ Total Protein - 24 - 25 g
- ⇒ Calcium - 90 mg (Leaves)
- ⇒ Thiamine (both) - 0.9 mg
- ⇒ Riboflavin (both) - 0.14 mg
- ⇒ Iron - 4 mg (leaves)
- ⇒ Calcium - 65 mg (seeds)
- ⇒ Energy - 1.18 MJ (seeds)

The % composition of amino acids within the cowpea protein is as follows - Range (average)

1) Lysine 5.7 - 9.6 (6.6)

2) Cystine 0.7 - 1.7 (0.9)

3) Methionine 0.7 - 1.6 (0.9)

4) Histidine 2.7 - 4.0 (3.3)

5) Threonine 3.4 - 5.3 (4)

6) Tryptophan 0.6 - 1.6 (0.9)

9.09 PROCESSING AND USES OF COWPEAS

Both cowpea leaves and seeds are eaten. Being a traditional crop, only traditional methods of Africa are known as far as processing is concerned. Some of these techniques are:

a) Leaves: Are plucked, cut into smaller pieces boiled for at least 30 minutes then fried. Either Odi from groundnuts or butter from churned milk could be added. This was a delicacy among the Luo, Luhya and the Mji Kenda of Kenya. The cowpea could be prepared alone or in combination of a number of traditional vegetable normally branded 'weeds' by agriculturalists.

b) Leaves: These could be washed, cut into pieces and then sun dried. After being packed in bags, these could store for weeks and even months. When to be cooked, they could be soaked in water for some time or just boiled and treated as in (a) above.

c) Pulses: The seeds could be used for making Nyoyo by the Luo. The traditional Nyoyo was boiled to softness mixture of sorghum and cowpea seeds. Later, maize replaced sorghum, and beans slowly replaced cowpeas when the production and popularity of the original two crops started dwindling.

d) Pulses: The seeds could be used for making Dengu. This was thoroughly boiled and fried seeds of cowpeas. The dish could then be eaten with Ugali.

9.10 PRODUCTION STATISTICS/DATA

Africa has been producing at least 60% of the total global cowpeas. In 1970, for instance it produced 93%. The total global production then was around 1,222,220 tons. Of this total production, Nigeria produced the bulk 60.2%, Niger 12.7%, Upper Volta 8.1% and Uganda 5.9%. The rest of Africa produced about 6.1% and other parts outside Africa produced 7%.

There are however a lot of doubts as to the accuracy of the African data. The crop has traditionally been both a multi-purpose and an inter-crop. Thus whereas the yields in West Africa is estimated to be 375 kg/ha, this can be gross underestimation. There are also lots of unreported plantings where the crop is produced largely for subsistence. This is a case in point in Eastern Africa - Kenya, Sudan, Ethiopia, and Tanzania etc where the crop originated. In West Africa, the reporting could be attributed to the fact that the crop is right now commercially produced. It is obvious that there has been a general bias towards commercial crops at the expense of subsistence crops. Hence the discrepancies in reporting.

Kenya produced 79,000t in 1992 and set a target production of 87,030 t for 1996. The global production in 1990 has been about 10,000,000 tons.

9.10 RESEARCH AND REQUIREMENTS OF COWPEAS

Kenya's KARI places cowpeas as the 29th crop out of 52 in order of research prioritization. It is surprising that with the great untested and unimproved nutritional and climatic potentials of cowpeas, it can be rated so poorly. It is known that Africa gets the bulk if any at all, its agricultural research funds from outside - the North. The source of the funds dictates the nature of research to be undertaken. Thus a lot of agricultural research is not to the interest of Africans themselves even though their own highly trained personnel are deployed there. There is a need to refocus the research priorities to consider as a matter of urgency the traditional foods that remain largely neglected and despised. For cowpeas, there is need to increase its production and consumption and improving its distribution and purchasing power of many Kenyans who remain below poverty line. The high energy and calorific density of cowpea, beans and groundnuts should put them much at the top agenda in agricultural research in this country.

There is therefore an immediate need for cowpea research in the following areas;

⇒ Processing techniques of the hard leaves, which in

most cases are wasted.

⇒ Keeping techniques for both leaves and pulses so that they can reach a wider market.

⇒ Increasing digestibility of the cowpea leaves

⇒ Processing techniques for seeds so as to reach a wider market.

It will be hard for Africa to develop as long as it does not give production and research priority to its own indigenous crops, foods and resources.

BIBLIOGRAPHY.

1. Abbott J.C. and Makeham. Agricultural Economics and marketing in the tropics. Longman scientific and technical, Hongkong.
2. Afullo O, Danga B, Adhiambo, H (1994). Background socio-economic survey report of the marginal areas of the Lake Victoria basin, INDICRECE, Kisumu. Pp 1-10.
3. Alan King (1985) Agriculture: An introduction for Southern Africa Cambridge University Press, Cambridge
4. Alila, Patrick O. (1979), Higher levels of agricultural production: Role of least developed farmers. IDS, UON.
5. Anyanzo L. (1988) Farm equipment, Machinery, Structures and buildings. East African Educational Publishers, Nairobi.
6. Areader,1989, Integrated management of Resources in Africa.1st edition,
7. Arthur, Thomas (1967). Farming in hot climates. 1st edition Faber & Faber Ltd. London pp 28-82.
8. Atieno Odhiambo, Ouso T I and Williams J F M (1985). A history of East Africa. Longman, London. Pp 1-158.
9. Brandt Commission (1983), Common crisis-North and South,Cooperation for world recovery.WCED
10. Chambers Robert (1983) Rural development: Putting the last first. Longman scientific & Technical, Newyork. Chapters 1-8.
11. Chengeta J and Matlhare C (1998) Enjoy Agriculture Book 1. Hodder and Stoughton.
12. Clariana, Roy B. 1982, Teaching Biology in Kenya: A Biology practical manual.
13. Cone, Wilson and Lipscomb J F (1972). History of Kenyan agriculture. University press of Africa, Nairobi. Pp 13-16.
14. Daily Nation, 23rd Jan, 4th Feb; 7th July; 9th, 10th, 11th and 13th Sept' 1993.
15. Elliot I (1997) Agriculture: A practical course for Botswana Book 3. Longman, Botswana.
16. Elliot I (1997) Agriculture: A practical course for Botswana Book 2. Longman, Botswana.
17. Elliot I (19977. Elliot I (1997) Agriculture: A practical course for Botswana Book 1 Longman, Botswana.
18. Elliot I (1998) Agriculture: A practical course. Book 1 Longman, Botswana.
19. Elliot RI, Stout GW, Dejardin EJ and Sithole DS (1998) Agriculture for Southern Africa: A practical approach upto Õ Level. Bell & Hyman in Association with Academic Books Zimbabwe, LONDON
20. FAO (1996). (unknown title: Tropical soils biology and fertility unit). FAO, Rome.

21. FAO of the UN (1991) FAO/Netherlands conference and the environment,
22. Fernie, John and Spitketh, Alan S. (1985) Resources: Environment and Policy. Herper and Row publishers.
23. Friedland, J. Andrew, 1989, Readings on Environmental issues in Kenya, Environment and Development. A report on Dartmouth College 1989 Kenya Environmental Studies Foreign Study Program, Dartmouth Foreign study Program, USA.
24. GOK (1986). Sessional paper no. 1: Economic management for renewed growth. Government printers, Nairobi. Pp 1-61.
25. GOK (1989) Siaya district Development plan. Government printers, Nairobi. Pp 1-30.
26. GOK (1989) South Nyanza district Development plan. Government printers, Nairobi. Pp 1-69.
27. GOK (1994) National Development plan. Government printers, Nairobi. Pp 5-9.
28. GOK (1994) Siaya district Development plan. Government printers, Nairobi. Pp 5-9.
29. GOK (1994) South Nyanza district Development plan. Government printers, Nairobi. Pp 5-9.
30. GOK (1994). Kenya farm management plan. Government printers, Nairobi.
31. GOK/ Government of Kenya, 1989/93 National Dev. Plan Ministry of National planning and Development, Government Printers.
32. Henry E. (1987). Soil conservation. College press Ltd, Harare, Zimbabwe.
33. Hill DS, Waller JM. (1992). Pests and diseases of tropical crops. Volume 1. Principles and methods of control. Longman group Limited., Essesx.
34. Humphreys L R. (1978). Tropical pastures and fodder crops. Longman group Limited, Hongkong.
35. IGAAD (1990) (Unknown title). IGAAD, Nairobi
36. Jackson R and Hutchinson C (1996). Gardening. Harper Collins Publishers, London.
37. KIE 1991, Secondary Agriculture: Form 3 pupils Book. Kenya Literature Bureau.
38. KNAS/ Kenya National Academy of Sciences (1988), Indigenous technologies of Kenya. 1st edition. KNAS.
39. Kotschi, Ann Waters; Bayer, Reinhard Adelhelm and Johanes, Ulrich Hoelse (1989). Ecofarming in agricultural development: Tropical agroecology 2, Verlagjosef margraf scientific books/GTZ.
40. Lenilian J and Fletcher W (1977)(eds). Environment and man: Vol 6 in the chemical environment. Blackie, Glasgow and London.

41. Leslie S Cobley (1976). An introduction to the botany of tropical crops 2nd edition, Longman, Newyork pp 1-59.

42. Lester R. Brown (1987) State of the world Report on Progress towards sustainable society, Worldwatch Institute.

43. Madeley, John (1991) When aid is no help: How projects fail and how they could succeed. (1st edition).Intermediate technology Publications, London

44. Middleton N (1988). Atlas of Environmental issues. Oxford University Press, Oxford.

45. Migori D.D.P., 1989/93 Migori District Development Plan, Ministry of National planning and Development, Government Printers.

46. Moran FT. (1992). Success in Vegetable and fruit production. Longman Zimbabwe.

47. Muchira SG and Ernelholm N. (1989) Agriculture for secondary Schools: A four year course> Heinemann Kenya

48. Ngugu DN, Karau PK and Nguyo W (1990) East African Agriculture

49. OAU (1980), Lagos Plan of Action for the economic Development of Africa.

50. Obara D and Ogonda R (1990). Kenya Secondary School Atlas. McMillan Kenya, Nairobi.

51. Odada J and OtienoJ (eds)(1990) Socio-economic profiles. GOK and Unicef, Nairobi. Pp 121 – 146.

52. Owen G (1984) O-Level Agriculture. Longman group Limited, London.

53. Roger Van (1972) The Agricultural history of Kenya. Historical Association of Kenya, Paper # 1. East African Publishing House, Nairobi. Pp 1-89.

54. Sakira WA (1981). Ó Level Agriculture. Oxford University Press Nairobi

55. Siaya D.D.P., 1989/93 Siaya District Development Plan, Ministry of National planning and Development, Government Printers.

56. Srinivasan, T. N. (1977), Development, poverty and Basic human needs:some issues. (1st edition) World Bank reprint series No. 76.

57. Srinivasan, T. N. (1981), Malnutrition: Some measurement and policy issues. World Bank reprint series No. 178.

58. The East African Standard, 23rd, Oct. 1993

59. The East African Standard, 23rd, Oct. 1997

60. UNEP (1985) State of the environment (2nd edition): Environmental aspects of emerging agricultural technologies; Population and the environment. UNEP.

61. USAID 1986, Kenya development strategy statement for 1986.

62. Watson M J (1983) Agriculture for Botswana. Macmillan Educational and the Ministry of Education, Botswana. London.

63. WCED / World Commission on environment and Development, 1987. Sustainable Development - a guide our common future.

64. White H P (1971). Commercial agriculture in tropical Africa. 1st edition. Hichs Smith & Sons Ltd. Wellington. Pp 10 – 35.

65. WRI (World Resources Institute), UNEP, UNDP, and world bank (1996). World resources: A guide to the global environment. WRI.

66. Yusuf A. (1981) Mechanisation. UNEP. Nairobi.

www.ingramcontent.com/pod-product-compliance
Lightning Source LLC
Chambersburg PA
CBHW071404290426
44108CB00014B/1678